CREATING CIRCLES OF POWER & MAGIC

A WOMAN'S GUIDE TO SACRED COMMUNITY

by
Caitlin Libera

The Crossing Press, Freedom, CA 95019

Library of Congress Cataloging-in-Publication Data

Libera, Caitlin.
    Creating circles of power & magic: a woman's guide to sacred
community / by Caitlin Libera.
        p.   cm.
    Includes bibliographical references
    ISBN 0-89594-713-7. —ISBN 0-89594-712-9 (pbk.)
    1. Copper Key (Coven)   2. Witchcraft—United States.   3. Women—
Religious life—United States—Case studies.   I. Title.   II. Title: Creating
circles of power and magic.
BF1578.C66L53 1994
299—dc20   94-20558
                                                                          CIP

Dedicated to the Women of Copper Key and their Families, with gratitude and appreciation for the gifts of their time, talents, experience, and friendship.

__Special thanks__ to Ginger Webber for her support and vision; to Mer-Nuit Amber for her commitment to Pagan civil rights and her research assistance on Chapter 9; to Tara and Orchid for their courage; to Pat & Eva for their editorial assistance; to Foxfire and Hannah; to D.F.C. & J.P.L. (may you both find happiness on your paths); to Pannayote for the cave; to River for her steadfast dedication to the Craft and her fellow Pagans; and to Laurel & Seal for their endless encouragement and faith. Blessed Be.

TABLE OF CONTENTS

GROUP EXERCISES

GLOSSARY OF TERMS

1
AN
INTRODUCTION

WHY THIS BOOK
WAS WRITTEN

DO YOU have a yearning to celebrate the seasons, to celebrate life in all its phases? Do you feel empowered to take charge of your own life and live it as if every action counted? Do you see the sacred in the mundane? Do you find ways to take yourself out of the city and into Nature, and do you feel reverence and awe in the face of Nature's beauty? Do you find yourself more and more in sync with the rhythms of the Moon, the tides, the Earth?

You may be on the verge of discovering (or you may have known for some time) that your own religious, spiritual beliefs are in line with what some people call Earth-Centered Spirituality, Women's Spirituality, Eco-Spirituality, Alternative Spirituality. Have you begun to define Deity in terms of that spirituality?

For most European-Americans who find themselves on this journey, the term "Witch" becomes the term with which they self-identify. It may come as a surprise, but Witchcraft is the broad term which is applied to any of the original Nature religions of Europe which predate Christianity. Self-identifying as a Witch is an homage to the women (and men) who have gone before, some giving their very lives for the right to believe and to worship as they have been called. Some prefer the term Wiccan, from Old English for *wise woman* or from the verb meaning *to bend or change,* from which the word Witch was derived. Others prefer to be called Goddess-Worshippers, or simply Pagans, meaning any of a huge population on Earth that have not given themselves to a hierarchical, organized religion imposed by the state or by societal pressures. And most believe that they have been born to believe this way, that their path for this lifetime is a path taking them away from mainstream religions.

Regardless of how you might self-identify, you may be yearning for people with whom to share your beliefs, people with whom to share the journey—a group to worship together, to learn together, to walk together. Some people call this group a Circle; some prefer a term from the Latin word for *to be of one mind, to agree, to come together:* a Coven. This word came into use during the Middle Ages, when the Inquisition was looking to persecute a group for every individual they accused of practicing Witchcraft. However, a modern definition is in order. In her book *The Spiral Dance*, Starhawk succinctly describes the place a Coven serves in the lives of Wiccans, Witches, and Pagans:

> *"The Coven is a Witch's support group, consciousness-raising group, psychic study center, clergy-training program, College of Mysteries, surrogate clan, and religious congregation rolled into one. In a strong Coven, the bond is, by tradition, 'closer than family': a sharing of spirits, emotions, imagination. 'Perfect love and perfect trust' are the goals."[1]*

Whether you wish to reclaim terms like Witch and Coven or not, the spiritual needs which can be met by a group along with the need for support and community will more than likely send every Pagan in search of a Circle at some point along the way.

Now more than ever, many women (and men) recognize the need for enlightened people to come together for fellowship. As we approach the 21st century, communities everywhere seem to have fallen by the wayside. Everyone from politicians to psychologists blame the lack of extended family for the problems that face our society. But there are those out there who are willing to recreate a nurturing spiritual environment for themselves and their families—this book is about women who came together to celebrate Wicca and found themselves creating community.

The focus is on a group of women from many different walks of life who have a Coven in common: it is called Copper Key. Most of the women have reclaimed the word Witch from the negative usage into which it has fallen and also use the term Coven to signify the

---

[1] Starhawk, THE SPIRAL DANCE, © 1989, HarperSan Francisco.

Circle in which they worship. Using interviews, surveys, and the members' own essays, this book will introduce the reader to each member of the coven; she is someone you may know, and you might even identify with her. All the members are well-educated, productive, sensitive women who happen to live a religious life quite unlike any the general public might recognize.

For the reader who is looking for the bonds of community and the expression of faith and trust that is a Coven, this book should serve as a manual of sorts for the creation of your own Circle. There are numerous books on the subject of Wicca, the faith, its rituals, practices, and teachers (reading recommended by the women themselves is included with each chapter); this text will distinguish itself from these other books by virtue of being a case study of one group that succeeded and became a practicing Coven.

Pagans and non-Pagans, Wiccans and Wiccan-curious, ethnologists and scholars, even critics of the New Age will find this text an honest and in-depth exploration of group dynamics. Through the accounts of the women who have taken the risk and through group exercises, personal inventories, and practical scripts, anyone contemplating the journey will be well prepared.

It is said that a person who wishes to define herself or himself as a Witch must study for at least a year-and-a-day; in Pagan ceremonies, a couple must spend a year-and-a-day together before they can be Handfasted (married); and a Circle must meet together for at least a year-and-a-day before they can call themselves a Coven. Enjoy the discovery.

AN INTRODUCTION TO WITCHCRAFT

"Now, on Tuesday, 19 July, came the decisive event for which so many in Massachusetts had been praying, a mass execution of the witches. Five were hanged on Gallows Hill, all women, the five whose trials had begun in late June: Rebecca Nurse, Goody Good, Elizabeth How, Sarah Wild, Susanna Martin."[1]

Perhaps in this day in the United States, people may rest more easily than they did in 1692; it is unlikely that anyone will be accused of Witchcraft and made to stand trial for sins against the Christian God. It is estimated that 90% of all people who died because of the Church's attempts to stamp out the Old Religion were not even associated with the Craft—rather, they were widows who owned property that would revert to the state upon their deaths, or midwives who continued to practice after men took over medicine, or women and men who opposed the iron rule of the Church, or just people unlucky enough to be fingered as a Witch by a neighbor with whom they had a quarrel.

It is believed that true practitioners of Witchcraft, or the Old Religion, went underground. In the general population, beliefs from the Old Religion about various Goddesses and Gods, holidays and celebrations, herbal remedies and healing, etc., were either translated into Christianity or relegated to "folk stories" and "old wives tales."

---

[1] Starkey, Marion L., THE DEVIL IN MASSACHUSETTS, Alfred A. Knopf, Inc., © 1949.

Today, thousands of women and men around the world are bringing the Old Religion back into the realm of spirituality, worship, and ways of life. They are discovering the wisdom of their foremothers and forefathers and putting it back into a place of honor in their lives. However, anyone who practices the religion of their ancestors— *Wiccecraft,* The Craft, Wicca, *Stregaria,* Paganism—must contend with the stigma of the popular associations of Witchcraft, and must also fight for the freedom to practice a religion of their own choosing in safety.

Each Halloween, homes and stores around the U.S. decorate their windows with green-faced women in pointy hats riding brooms. The evil antagonists in fairy tales are witches ready to eat little children. Just a few years ago, ABC Television shot a pilot called *The Craft.* Subsequent shows would have featured a woman running with her newborn to save it from the clutches of a coven of Witches that sought to kidnap it and raise it to be their Witch leader; luckily, public outcry kept the show off the air (due in great part to Circle Network News, published by Circle Sanctuary).

Modern Witches, such as the ones you will meet in this book, are women and men who want the Western world to realize that regardless of the stereotypes associated with the Craft, they have the right to practice the religion of their choice. Basically, religions that are considered Witchcraft encompass the following beliefs:

- Deity is both male and female.
- Polytheism (belief and worship of many Goddesses and Gods).
- A reverence for Nature and the Earth, and a belief that all life is interconnected; the elements Earth, Air, Fire, and Water are revered.
- Belief that all personal actions will be returned three times over, whether they be good or bad deeds, thoughts, or speech.
- One is free to do as one pleases, as long as *no one else is harmed* in any way; even if one has good intentions, any harm which may come to pass is the responsibility of the individual.
- Every person affects what comes to pass in her/his life.
- Deity may speak or work through all people and things.
- People of all ethnicities, races, genders, and religions are equal.
- All life is sacred.

The following questions are frequently asked about modern Witchcraft:

CAN WITCHES CAST SPELLS TO MAKE SOMEONE LOVE THEM? DO THEY MAKE BAD THINGS HAPPEN TO PEOPLE THEY DON'T LIKE? COULD I GIVE THEM MONEY TO CAST A SPELL ON SOMEONE?

Any persons who purport to use their personal power to dominate another person, to get revenge, to curse someone, or to do any of the things popular fiction associates with the power of Witchcraft, are not following the Old Religion. Any act which encroaches upon the free will of another human being without that person's consent is against the tenets of the faith. The question, "Are you a good Witch or a bad Witch?" has no place in the true practice of the Craft. Those who claim to be "black Witches" or to be "walking the Dark Path" are not included under the umbrella of the Old Religion, Witchcraft, or Paganism. Money is never exchanged for any act of magic on behalf of another person by true Witches.

DO WITCHES WORSHIP SATAN?

On the question of Satanism, here are the facts: modern-day Witches *do not believe* in the existence of a supreme good or a supreme evil; the dichotomy of God versus Satan is a purely Judeo-Christian invention, and one that Witches believe is much younger than the religion that they practice. Satanism as a religion does exist, but it is believed that Satanism was not even practiced before the mid-1800s. Unfortunately, everything outside the accepted Judeo-Christian ethic is linked to Satanism by the uneducated—and this linkage doubles the burden of modern Witches as they attempt to secure the rights afforded them under the constitutional guarantee of Freedom of Religion.

Some sources of misinformation claim that there are levels of Wicca which lead progressively to Satan as individuals are initiated into higher and higher levels of an order; the women of this book believe that the only initiator is oneself—there are no hierarchical levels of advancement. Of the formal systems with which these women are familiar, none of the Priests or Priestesses of their acquaintance are associated with Satanism in any way.

One reason the ancient European religions (the Old Religions) are so often connected to Satanism is that the medieval Catholic Church personified Satan with the characteristics of the Pagan Horned God—Pan in Greece, Faunus in Italy, Herne in Great Britain, the Celtic Cernunnos—in order to associate Pagans with the nemesis of everything holy and thereby stamp out the Old Religions, which were in direct competition with the Church for resources. These Pagan Gods are associated with hunting and were horned because they represented not only the hunter but also the prey.

IS WITCHCRAFT A CULT?

Cults today are defined by several specific items about their practice: a very strong central personality generally dominates the religion or the sect; members are required to give up a good deal of their personal identity for the good of the group; finances, contact with family and friends, and a person's sex life will come under the control of the group or the central character; techniques of brainwashing, such as sleep or sensory deprivation, may be used to keep converts in line; finding new converts is a major goal of the group.

Cults can spring up in any religious community, including Christianity—Wicca is much less likely to be involved with cult behavior because it is a religion the central focus of which is individual responsibility; proselytism (seeking converts) is frowned upon; ethics of Witchcraft hold that teachers and religious leaders cannot accept money in exchange for information or membership in a group. Wiccans believe that each person is born with a specific path to follow in this lifetime, and that individuals find their way to that path on their own, whether it be Wicca, Buddhism, Shintoism, Catholicism, or any other spirituality. However, *any* group which tries to dominate a member in areas of finance, sex, isolation, or even habitat should be considered dangerous. It is important to remember that Jim Jones could just as easily have claimed to be a Wiccan as a Christian; it was his sick desire for power rather than his spiritual beliefs that led to the deaths of so many people.

DO WITCHES PRACTICE ANIMAL OR HUMAN SACRIFICE?

No. If all life is sacred, and all life comes from the Goddess and God, there is no need for blood sacrifice. Modern Witches do not offer these sacrifices in any rituals they perform.

"Libations" are offered to the Gods: this means pouring the first sip of wine or juice and the first bite of cake or bread out on the ground in thanks for the bounty provided (Wiccans who are very strict about this practice also prepare a libation at every meal).

The question does persist about possible human and/or animal sacrifice in the true ancient practice of the Old Religions; ancient references to sacrifices in Europe indicate that the "victim" volunteered for the duty so that a drought might end, or so that a harvest might come in, or because the cycle called for it. Symbolic sacrifices, such as a doll made of corn to look like a man, were often used instead. However, it should be noted that many rituals in the Old Testament required animal sacrifice, and Christians today do not follow those practices, either.

While a more complete glossary can be found at the end of this book, the following terms are used throughout the text. Their meanings affect comprehension of the story of Copper Key:

Wicca: the religion of modern Witches, from the Old English word for *wise;* a practitioner may call herself or himself a Wiccan, a Witch, or a Pagan (both male and female practitioners are called Witches — the word 'warlock' is a medieval Christian invention).

Craft, The: an umbrella term for all traditions of Witchcraft; a person practices The Craft if she or he is a Wiccan or a Witch.

Circle: may refer to: 1) a group who meets for religious worship (also, a group who has not yet taken Covenstead will often be referred to as a Circle; 2) the space in which Wiccans/Witches meet to worship; 3) "Circling" refers to the practice of meeting together for worship.

Coven: a group of Wiccans/Witches who have been meeting together for at least a year-and-a-day.

Covenstead: a formal declaration or ritual which designates a Circle as a practicing Coven.

Tradition: the particular type of Paganism a person practices; one often hears, "In our tradition," when Wiccans speak of their own beliefs and practices.

Pagan: any person who practices any one of the religions of aboriginal peoples who have been conquered by or been forced into conformance to Christianity; Druidism, Wicca, and Native American spirituality are all examples of Pagan religions.

Magic: power to manifest change at will; while works of magic may be short-term and specific (i.e., a spell to get a job, to put a hole in a cloud to hold off a thunderstorm, or for the willpower to quit smoking), real magic is living in and maintaining a state of harmony and balance with the continual changes of life.

Spell: a focus of attention on a specific goal; equivalent of "praying" for a specific outcome; some spells are complete with props and actions to aid in focusing individual or group attention on the goal— others are silent wishes.

Eclectic: a belief system or practice drawn from many different sources or traditions; a person or group may be referred to as 'eclectic' or as 'an eclectic.'

Wheel, The: generally a term referring to the Wheel of the Year, a Pagan calendar consisting of the lunar cycles and Sabbats and Solstices; it is a microcosm of the Wheel of Life, from birth through death and rebirth.

USING THIS BOOK

THERE IS perhaps no other religion which relies more heavily on intuition than Wicca. For this reason, readers who are seeking a spiritual life that is both attainable and comfortable for themselves must become actively involved with the texts which they rely upon for information.

At the end of each chapter you will find a page entitled *Journal Entries.* There will be several topics and questions from which to choose, and they are designed to help you find the tip of the iceberg of your own emotions, thoughts, wants, needs, fears, and beliefs. You will need a blank book, anything from a school notebook to one of the fancy cloth-bound journals you see now in bookstores all over the country. The Crossing Press also publishes illustrated journals, such as Irene Zahava's *Moonflower: A Book of Affirmations.* Ask your favorite purveyor of books to help you find something perfect for you. And then use it. Set aside at least thirty minutes each day just for you and your writing.

When you meet with a new group, or make a contact, or attend a seminar, a gathering, or a public ritual, be sure to get your emotions down in your journal while the experience is still fresh in your mind. This will become increasingly important the closer you get to joining a Circle or Coven, or taking Covenstead with your own Circle; your journal can be your best friend when it comes time to make decisions about your Craft life. Trusting yourself is an important factor in making the right decisions, but if you find yourself caught up in the moment or pressured in any way to make a commitment, look back to your journal: how did you feel when you first met these people? How happy have you been at subsequent meetings? Are there any questions that have not been answered to your satisfaction? There, in your own handwriting in your own journal, should be what you need to know to help you decide.

Once you have found a group, you should also plan to keep a journal of the meetings and the rituals and the events which occur. This is the beginning of your own magical journal, and possibly a "Book of Shadows" for your own Coven.

This book also contains ritual scripts, recommended reading, exercises, meditations, meeting suggestions, recipes, and advice from the members of the Copper Key Coven. Use these to help your own group get started, or modify them for use in your private practice. Experiment and discover the things which make you feel the most comfortable, those things which you will keep as part of your own tradition.

JOURNAL ENTRIES

1. Why did I choose to read this book?

2. If a member of my family, or my best friend, or my lover asked me to define my religious beliefs, this is what I would say:

3. This is my experience to date with Circles, Covens, and Pagan organizations:

4. Why am I interested in learning about Circles & Covens? Do I feel that I need support for my own beliefs? Am I looking for a community, a family, a support group, a networking resource?

5. These are the things that I hope to have learned by the time I finish this book:

COPPER KEY RECOMMENDS:

The Chalice & The Blade, by Riane Eisler; San Francisco: Harper & Row, ©1987.

Drawing Down the Moon, by Margot Adler; Boston: Beacon Press, ©1990 (2nd ed).

The Great Cosmic Mother, by Monica Sjöö & Barbara Mor; HarperSan Francisco, ©1991.

The Holy Book of Women's Mysteries, by Zsuzsanna Budapest; Berkeley: Wingbow Press, ©1989.

Moonflower: A Book of Affirmations, Irene Zahava, ed.; Freedom, California: The Crossing Press, ©1985.

The Spiral Dance, by Starhawk; HarperSan Francisco, ©1989.

The Witches' God, by Janet & Stewart Farrar; Custer, Washington: Phoenix Publishing, Inc., ©1989.

The Witches' Goddess, by Janet & Stewart Farrar; Custer, Washington: Phoenix Publishing, Inc., ©1987.

Fiction:

The Fifth Sacred Thing, by Starhawk; New York: Bantam Books, ©1993.

The Return of the Goddess, by Elizabeth Cunningham; Barrytown, New York: Station Hill Press, ©1992.

Sisters of the Dream, by Mary Sojourner; Flagstaff, Arizona: Northland Publishing, ©1989.

2
FINDING
THEIR WAY TO
COMMUNITY

LAUREL'S STORY

MY FATHER'S family is from the Delta, Mississippi Baptists. My mother's family were farmers from Virginia, Methodists. When my parents met, they became Methodists, and my siblings and I were raised that way. Even as a small child I thought it was kind of a wishy-washy religion; there was not much you could get your teeth into. We went to a church considered High Methodist: the minister wore a robe, and that's as much ritual as we got. I always felt a real envy of my friends who were Roman Catholics, but my father would have rather seen me dead at his feet than let me convert. When I was nineteen, I took the bit in my teeth and decided I was going to become an Episcopalian, and I did. I found that church very rewarding because it had a very rich ritualistic element with the incense, flags, statuary, and a special book of prayers; it had a lot of things to recommend it.

When I met and married Seal, we had all our children baptized in the Episcopal church and they went to an Episcopal school, but there was something that was not fulfilling about it. Right before my fortieth birthday, which was a watershed, I decided that my goal for the year was to figure out what it was I really did believe in spiritually and religiously. I wasn't too far into that thought process before I realized that I couldn't say the Apostles' Creed sincerely. I obviously didn't belong in the Episcopal Church, and so I started reading. I consulted a dear friend in seminary, who recommended some broad-spectrum, world religion books, and I casually asked her what she knew about the "Old Religion." She answered, "Starhawk came to speak to us at Divinity School. She was a very interesting woman, very articulate. I think you'll enjoy her book, *The Spiral Dance*." She wrote down several book titles for me, and about six weeks later I bought them all. *Spiral Dance* was the first one I read, and I know it's a cliché, but when I started reading it, it was like, "Oh, *this* is what it's called —well look at that, other people think that way, too." It was really exciting for me. When Seal and I were in bed one Sunday night I turned to him and said, "There's something I need to tell you. I've decided that what I really am is a Witch. Are you going to be able to deal with this?" He thought it was pretty strange, but he thought he could deal with it okay, and he did.

By the time my birthday rolled around, I had read all the books. For my birthday, Seal gave me a chalice because you should receive your chalice from someone who loves you, and I got my bell for the altar.

By this time, I was deep into it. I kept going into bookstores and clearing the shelves of anything that was even remotely touching on Witchcraft. I did my personal dedication[1] at the Blue Moon on New Year's Eve. I opened all the windows in my bedroom and turned off all the lights and sat in the moonlight and did my own dedication.

Soon afterward I went into a herb shop and got to talking with the salesperson—she recommended a fairly new women's bookstore. I went there and met the owner, who knew thousands of things I should read. I got on her mailing list for monthly events; one mailing mentioned that an hereditary Witch was to speak at the store. She and her family were giving a concert, a women's workshop, a men's workshop, and a drumming seminar. I called the store. I remember I was at the office and I closed the door tightly before I picked up the phone. Bluntly I said, "So who's the Witch?" She explained the events to me, and I signed up.

After the morning women's workshop, everyone was still keeping to themselves, but after the drumming that night everyone really loosened up. Several of us exchanged phone numbers. Each woman told how long she had been practicing the Craft, and if she worked

---

[1] A ceremony or ritual in which a person makes a promise or vow to study a given tradition or religious system—it does not imply initiation but rather association and study.

with a group or alone. We tentatively decided to get together. I had all the women's telephone numbers at the end of the day.

Before the next Full Moon, I called some of the women. The owner of the bookstore had given us permission to meet there as a kind of a neutral meeting ground. We really didn't know each other well enough to go to someone's home. After having lined up these people I realized that I should figure out what it was that I was going to do as Priestess. I made an outline of a ritual I thought would be appropriate.

I called a woman who runs a local retreat center (she has a degree from Circle Sanctuary) to see if what I had planned sounded right. She said, "Now let me get this straight. You've never been a Priestess, you've never even been to a Circle, and you're leading this one?" When I said yes, she commented, "Where angels fear to tread..." But she thought my outline sounded all right, that I had covered all the bases.

That first night there must have been seven of us there. I don't think the Earth moved. I worked from notes (I didn't have a clue what I was going to say if it wasn't written down). It was a totally plagiarized ritual, straight out of all the books I had read, but everyone wanted to meet again. We met on Ostara next and the following Full Moon, and then we added New Moons.

We date the formation of the group from Ostara, although we did have that one Moon before. For well over a year-and-a-day we did not consider ourselves a Coven, but rather a group or a Circle, because we felt pretty strongly that Covenstead was something you achieved — you couldn't just say, "Okay, now we're a Coven."

By the time we decided we'd been through enough rising water and drought to be a Coven, it was July of the second year of meeting. There had been some turnover of membership. One Yule we had close to thirty people. Then we had a couple of scares. Some people felt that they were being forced out of the broom closet by other people who were thoughtless or indiscreet. Before the end of the first year we decided in order to preserve the privacy of the people involved, we would close the membership. Before that, we had a revolving, open-door policy.

At one time, we had thirteen members, an ideal number. Due to attrition, or people moving away, or deciding that their path was taking them away from Wicca, we've been as low as nine. But now, a year after we took Covenstead, we're back to twelve members.

CREATING A COMMUNITY OF YOUR OWN: MEET THE WOMEN OF COPPER KEY

"I THINK we've created a community," Laurel said. "We became a Circle first and then formed individual friendships, which may be contrary to the way it usually works, but I feel a tie to the group as a whole and a very strong tie to certain individuals within the group."

The diagram on the following page shows the women of the Copper Key Circle. The solid lines forming boxes represent women who took Covenstead, and broken lines indicate members who moved on before it occurred.

This diagram shows the way in which the women came into the group: i.e., Laurel called the first meeting and invited the women in the first row to attend. The people who found their way into the group through another person are listed under that person. For example, Mer-Nuit and Ginger met Foxfire at an open meeting at the Unitarian Universalist Church. They were, in turn, the point of contact for other women from the U. U. Church who eventually joined Copper Key as well.

There are close to thirty other women who met with the group over the three-year period which this book covers, but they were not the core members who stayed together and took responsibility for planning rituals, serving as Priestess, arranging retreats, and participating in decision-making.

Several of the members also studied with a national teaching coven, the Hidden Grove. This coven was at that time led by a couple who travelled the country meeting with small groups in many different cities. They met the women of Copper Key through seminars sponsored by the women's bookstore and by the sociology depart-

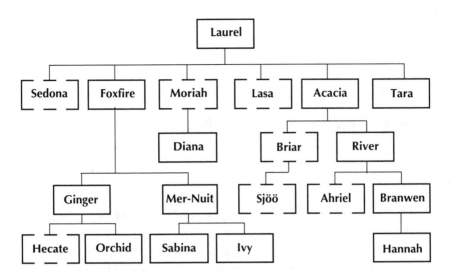

The Women of Copper Key

Solid boxes indicate members at the time of Covenstead; dashed lines indicate members of the Circle who left the group before that time. This graphic is designed to indicate how each woman originally made contact with the Circle. The top line of six are the women who attended the first meeting Laurel called, in February, 1991.

---

ment of the local university. Their interaction with Copper Key will be discussed throughout the text.

The women outlined above are either those who made significant contributions to the "herstory" of Copper Key or who figure prominently in the stories they tell about their first two years together. In addition to the founding mothers of the group, the reader will eventually meet Willow, the first member of the next generation of Copper Key, who joined the Circle in its third year of meeting together.

THE FIRST MEETING

THE FIRST meeting of the group that would become Copper Key was held at the bookstore which was central to all the women who eventually passed through the Circle's door. The owner entrusted Laurel with the key to her shop and showed her where she kept a green plastic tarp to cover the windows.

"Briar and I were supposed to go, but she was sick that day. I ended up going alone, and I was a little nervous," Acacia said. "Luckily I felt comfortable in the bookstore. No one said much at first, we just offered to help set up the room, move bookcases and whatnot, and Laurel went about setting up the ritual space. She seemed to know what to do: she had music playing on the tape deck of the store, and had Lasa laying out the boundaries of the Circle with smooth stones. She put a candle in each of the cardinal points on top of a larger rock."

Eventually, a little past the appointed meeting time, there were seven women assembled in the store. "When it came time to start, Laurel locked the door and we all sat on the floor inside the rocks, six of us in a semicircle facing Laurel," Acacia continued. "She knew that I was studying with Hidden Grove and asked me to sweep. When I went around the Circle three times with the broom, she was thrilled: it had never dawned on her that it was supposed to be done three times—the books apparently left that out."

Laurel led the group through Diane Mariechild's "Healing Stars" meditation.[1] After preparing them by asking that they close their eyes and sit comfortably, she began:

---

[1] Page 142, *Mother Wit: A Guide to Healing & Psychic Development,* by Diane Mariechild; Freedom, California: The Crossing Press, ©1981, 1988.

"Your body is strong. Your body is so strong that it can take care of itself. Your mind is strong. Your mind is so strong that it keeps your body well. Good energy is all around you. Every time you breathe, you breathe in good energy and it moves all through your body and it keeps your body well.

And now picture a big blue star over your head. A big blue star is over your head. Suddenly it bursts into thousands of tiny blue stars. A shower of stars pouring down on you. It is raining little blue sparkling stars. These tiny little stars are healing energy. When you take a deep breath, you bring the stars into your body. When you breathe out, all the little stars move through your body. All the tiny blue stars are moving through your body. You feel all warm and tingly as the stars move through your body. The blue stars are moving all through your body just like your blood does. They are moving into your toes and feet. They are moving up through your legs and hips. The blue stars are filling your stomach and your chest. You feel all warm and tingly as the tiny blue lights move along your back, all through your back, your shoulders, your neck. And now the tiny blue lights are moving into your head. The tiny blue lights will move all through your body all night, and when you wake up you will feel strong and well."

After the meditation Laurel passed out some tiny, star-shaped confetti for everyone to take home with them.

Tara said, "Then we did a short Full Moon ritual, and we talked about ourselves, who we were, where we were coming from, and whether we wanted to continue meeting. We were terrified of society as a whole. I don't want my house firebombed, I don't want to take on the Fundamentalist Christians. I do believe in the first amendment right to say and to believe what I want, but I don't want to have to act on that assumption. We were scared. But this was so important that we decided, 'Okay—let's try and do this again.' And all of us absolutely did not know what we were doing."

Acacia said, "At the end of the meeting, Laurel asked if I would serve as Priestess at the next meeting. I was not really sure I was ready to do that. I had seen a few rituals and had been studying for a little while, but was I ready to lead a ritual for a whole group of people? Laurel had a knack of making you feel as if you are just what the doctor ordered, and her enthusiasm and the group saying they wanted me to made me feel special and safe. I agreed to do it, and by the time we left that night, I wanted to do the best ritual anybody'd ever seen, because I knew these women deserved it. I immediately felt a sense of responsibility to the group, even though we hadn't even decided that we *were* a group yet."

Tara added, "That first meeting just felt right; we felt like we were at home. And I've been there ever since."

DEFINING RITUAL, MOON, SABBAT & SOLSTICE

RITUAL AND celebration served to bring the women of Copper Key together; friendship and trust allowed them to use the ritual space for healing, personal progress, and joy, all in the presence of the Gods. Their choice of Wicca as a way of life was reinforced by the sharing of Moons, Sabbats, Solstices, and other special rituals.

A Wiccan ritual serves to establish a place in this world for humans and Deity to meet. It is comprised of building a ritual space or temple, inviting in the Spirits of the Earth Elements, inviting in the Goddess and the God (or solely the Goddess, in the case of most Dianic traditions), celebrating the occasion, praying, meditating, raising energy, and thanking Deity. In these respects, it is not very different from other religious ceremonies: a church or synagogue is referred to as the house of the Lord; priests, ministers, and rabbis give an invocation; praying and thanking God occurs. Even if you have not yet been to a Wiccan ritual, you might imagine how it would feel to participate in a ritual as a priest, rabbi, or minister. What would you do?

"Acting as the Priestess will call out characteristics in a person that she didn't even know she had. Some of our most memorable rituals have been done by women who initially disavowed any talent in the direction of being Priestess at all," Laurel said. "They may not be the biggest mouth in the group, they may not be the first with an opinion, but they are very, very good Priestesses. In fact, I've never seen a bad Priestess in our group."

"I never really got into ritual until I was Priestess," Mer-Nuit added. "I never paid attention to what and why. Now I feel like I can put all the pieces together in my mind."

Perhaps the tradition of having thirteen members in a Coven stems from there being thirteen lunar cycles in the calendar year, and therefore one cycle over which each member may officiate. These cycles are celebrated on both the New and Full Moons by most Wiccan Circles, and Copper Key is no exception. They adopted rituals for the New and Full Moon from a variety of sources: a few came to be part of what some members call the Copper Key Tradition.

On New Moons, the time in the lunar cycle when new projects should be started, each member makes a vow to complete a given task before the following New Moon. The task can be something as complex as giving up smoking or something as mundane as "finishing the laundry" or "cleaning out the kids' closets." The act of vowing in front of the Gods and the entire Circle to complete or continue a certain task or behavior gives greater impetus to the members to actually do it. Also, the Circle members, by bearing witness to the vow, are committed to helping each member succeed.

In some traditions, Full Moons are times for making wishes. Generally, Copper Key members wish for things they need to achieve a particular goal (i.e., "I wish for all A's on finals"). The wishes are generally things that the member herself plays a part in making come true. Occasionally, someone might wish for the winning lottery ticket, or some other pie in the sky. However, the admonition that one be careful what one wishes for or one might just get it certainly applies here—according to Wiccan beliefs, if you simply wish for money or perform a ritual to that end, it is possible that a close relative might die and leave you heir to their wealth—do you want to shoulder that responsibility?

Responsibility for one's actions is probably more acute in Wicca than in the Judeo-Christian ethic, as each Wiccan must recognize her/his place in the grand scheme of things and the effect of will upon the future. This is not to say that the Gods don't often let someone know when they've made a wrong turn. One member of Copper Key entered every sweepstakes and wished on successive Moons to win. One day a package arrived at her front door: she had won. Opening the box, she was less than thrilled to find a baseball cap embroidered with a sweepstakes logo. It was, at the very least, a lesson in being specific.

Copper Key celebrated each of the eight Wiccan holidays (the Sabbats, made up of four mythological events plus the Solstices and Equinoxes) which occurred during their first year-and-a-day together. These celebrations were natural events around which to build weekend retreats or extended meetings. By planning and taking more time with these occasions, the Coven began to build its own traditions around the holidays and came to appreciate celebrating them with their new family.

The religious aspects of ritual, in the hands of the Priestesses of Copper Key, were the first thing that all the women had in common. It was because they came together to worship that they were able to put aside their worldly differences—socio-economic status, educational background, lifestyle choices—and build friendships that might not have grown outside this experience.

SUGGESTIONS FOR WOMEN IN SEARCH OF A CIRCLE OR COVEN

"IF YOU'RE going into a group new to you and someone from that group wants to meet you and asks you to come to his or her home, be careful," advises a police lieutenant. "Especially, a woman should view going into any group, I don't care if it's the Knights of Columbus, the Unitarian Church, the Roman Catholic Church, any group, as a potential rape situation. Just keep that in your mind. Religious people can be bad guys, too."

He travels the country offering seminars for law enforcement on alternative spirituality and the First Amendment guarantee for religious freedom. In his work he has to consider the potential physical danger involved when any person goes into an unknown situation; however, his advice applies to anyone looking for a group with which to Circle. Here are some suggestions for your first encounter with any new group or person:

- Meet in a public place.
- Try not to go alone.
- If you must go alone, let someone know where you're going and what time you should be home. Have a contact person—call her or him and say, "Hi, I'm leaving now, I'm supposed to be at this place, from this time to this time. I've never been there before. If you don't hear from me by 9:30, I'm in trouble."
- Check these people out. Say to yourself, "Am I comfortable with the looks of this person/these people?"
- Try to identify their car(s) and make a note of license plates.
- Any time that you're not comfortable, leave. If they won't let you leave, scream, yell, and make a commotion.

Hopefully, no one who wants to find a Circle, a Coven with which to practice, or a teacher of the Craft will need this information. Today, you never know what situation you may encounter.

Even after joining a Coven or Circle, you and your group may wish to adopt a policy on allowing visitors to ritual. While you may not be concerned with physical safety, many members of your group may not wish to be known publicly as Witches or Pagans. Members of Copper Key offered convincing arguments on why you may not want to go public, particularly in certain areas of the country. "Witches don't win custody fights, not in our time, unfortunately, regardless of what sort of person they may be," said Tara. While working toward the public acceptance of the Craft should be the goal of every member, some people are not able to throw caution to the wind and leap out of the broom closet. That is why, in fact, throughout this book you will only see the adopted Craft or Circle names of members of the Copper Key Coven. Craft names are said to have been handed down through the ages for insuring the safety of its members; in some Circles, only Craft names are *ever* used. These names can also serve to represent the fact that by joining a Coven you are in essence being adopted by a new family, and you may choose a name to designate that distinction (see Appendix 1 for a group exercise on names).

To insure the safety of the group, Copper Key designated one member who was somewhat comfortable with being known publicly as a Witch to meet prospective new members at a restaurant or other public place prior to inviting that person to attend a Circle, although this policy was not adopted until the beginning of their second year of meeting together. "There's a tendency toward an open door policy when you first find Wicca," said Laurel, when asked what one aspect of the Coven experience she would warn other groups about. "You tend to get real evangelical about it. You may not mean to go out and proselytize, but you get so excited about having found a group that you want to spread the wealth. You want to let anyone who's even remotely interested come try it, because it's been so wonderful for you."

Unfortunately, Laurel found herself recognized publicly (and loudly) by an overzealous young man who had attended a Yule celebration. Although guests were welcome and Laurel had served as Priestess, this guest had not thought through the consequences of his hearty greeting to her in a restaurant. Her dining party did not know about her Craft involvement. Whenever your group decides to bring in a new member, or when a person who may be shopping for a group asks to visit, or when you wish to celebrate a holiday with family or friends in a ritual, the guests must be made aware that the privilege is not without responsibility—and that responsibility is the tactful regard for the reputations of the members of the Circle.

JOURNAL ENTRIES

1. In what type of environment would I feel most comfortable learning and worshiping?

2. After reading Laurel's Story, this is how I felt:

3. These are the questions that will be important for me to ask when I call a bookstore or the library about Pagan groups that have public meetings:

4. How comfortable am I with people of different backgrounds, ethnicities, and/or sexual orientations? I will honestly evaluate my own feelings, and try to consider how I might feel meeting with a group in which I might be a minority.

5. What things would I like a group to provide me with, and what things would I willingly provide to a Circle? What must I absolutely have to make the experience worthwhile?

COPPER KEY RECOMMENDS:

The Goddess Celebrates, by Diane Stein; Freedom, California: The Crossing Press, © 1991.

Mother Wit: A Guide to Healing & Psychic Development, by Diane Mariechild; Freedom, California: The Crossing Press, © 1988.

3
LEADERSHIP
& LEARNING

ACACIA'S STORY

I HAVE tried to remember how it was before, during those long years of Catholicism. I never believed women were inherently responsible for original sin, but I found the act of praying, the ritual of mass, comforting. I never thought that only a man in a confessional box could speak to God on my behalf to ask for forgiveness. But there I went, week after week, confessing my unworthiness.

I never knew a priest well enough to speak to him about my *real* life. For that matter, no nun ever filled the role of confidant, either. I connected with the image of Mary, the Virgin Mother, very strongly. It was to her that I addressed my prayers, begging for her intercession with Jesus and God and all the others who were supposedly too lofty and unapproachable for a mere mortal sinner like me. And I, of course, knew that I had to stave off anger, reject the hormones of youth, turn the other cheek, be quiet and then be rewarded in heaven. I never told an adult that life in my house was a nightmare. I always believed that Mary and the Catholic church wouldn't lie to me — that I would truly be better off for suffering. I knew the Beatitudes and said them over and over when my alcoholic father was violent.

I was truly saved when in college I finally found an adult in whom I could confide the truth. I learned that God did not expect me to be beaten in order to be a good person; I found out that other children of alcoholics existed and that they were scared and ridiculed by their parents and afraid, too. That was the first time that I consciously considered that maybe this man-centered religion was not telling the whole truth. The 12-Step concept of a Higher Power, in which I turned my will over to God *as I understood God,* meant that I had the freedom to accept or reject the religious doctrine that I had been spoon-fed since childhood. It was a concept that began to give me back a little of the personal power that had been drained out of me.

The first time I heard another twelve-stepper say "Goddess" instead of "God," I seriously thought he was a flake. I mean, goddesses were romantic notions from Latin class. Who would call the Higher Power "she" and mean it? Whom was this guy trying to impress? However, to hear a man express his understanding of God as *she* gave me pause for thought.

Over a period of several years, I began to think more and more about Nature, and the "man was created in His own image and likeness" stories. If that were so, why are we not all hermaphrodites? Where in Nature (above single-celled organisms) does procreation take just one?

Being more a student than a philosopher, I began looking for the exceptions. OK, legend has it that there could have been a tribe of women, Amazons, who were genetically capable of parthenogenesis (reproducing without fertilization by a partner — two eggs combining to create a fetus). And, as the gametes would only contain genetic material from one woman, the offspring would be female and prone to the same genetic specialty. A stretch, yes, but a potential.

Was there any similar case for the male gender? I'm still looking. Men are not built to give birth. And all this time, I have been programmed to believe that a male god gave rise to the entire universe!

The myths from Latin class began preying on my mind. Yes, children supposedly sprang from Zeus's head and his leg. But where did Zeus come from?

A-ha! Imagine my surprise when I finally got a clear picture in my head of how the Olympians came into being. The original being, the original presence, was a *female* who consisted of all matter and energy, who, upon becoming aware of herself, gave birth to a companion; a male. Their union brought forth the universe, and their children were gods and goddesses.

So, this was one story in which a woman was first. Were there more? Over and over, in each culture's mythology, there was the Mother and the strong womanspirit. Even in Judaism, Lilith, who has since been relegated to the "Dark Side" and called evil, was really just a female figure who would not be dominated by a male god. In each culture, with time the male gender subverted the role of the woman. War and conquest supplanted the cyclical birth-life-death-rebirth of the Goddess as the natural order of things.

Some of the aboriginal religions which are still practiced today have not yet turned away from the Mother. That gave me hope. Surely there was someone who knew the religion of my ancestors in Europe.

No one was more surprised than I to learn that these religious practices are considered Witchcraft. More than a little intrigued, I began looking for discreet ways to buy books on the subject. I even sought out the so-called occult shops, in the guise of searching for decorations for a Halloween party. I began encountering people who ranged from bizarre to normal to extremely interesting. But I still wasn't going to go public with my intent to become a practitioner of the Old Religions.

After incorporating a good bit of herbalism into my daily life, altering my observance and celebration of various holidays, and frequenting stores and shops which sold organically grown foods, environmentally friendly products, and cruelty-free cosmetics, I still felt like a puzzle with missing pieces. I had half the picture, maybe less, but I didn't know where to go for help. Many of my 12-Step friends held very tightly to traditional Judeo-Christian beliefs; one went so far as to tell me openly that if I wasn't Christian the program couldn't work for me.

My husband, who considers himself an analytical, intellectual atheist, knew me well enough to recognize that I was in need of the kind of community support for my religious beliefs as I had found for my recovery in Adult Children Of Alcoholics. There was a group of students at the college where he was on the faculty who had started a Pagan Student Union; he introduced me to one of its more vocal members. It just so happened that this woman was a student of Wiccan teachers who traveled the country, and whose extended Coven included hundreds of people in cities across the U.S. She offered to let me listen to the teaching tapes which they distributed, and, as they were due in our town within a few weeks, invited me to participate in a Circle when they arrived.

Again, my husband encouraged me, although the prospect of real Witches made him a little nervous. We listened to the first tape together. There were many things which seemed foreign, but also many things which felt familiar to me and moreover made sense. The tape made it clear that this group was not after money or looking for converts; the members promised to teach anyone if he or she promised to learn; beyond that, there was no commitment expected. My husband was not inclined to attend himself, and he was more than a little anxious about my going, but in the end we both decided that I would go.

I met my first Pagans in an old house. I went up a narrow staircase to a small room where they were staying during their visit. I was more nervous than I previously thought. The whole time I spent with them had a very unreal, out-on-the-edge feeling, as if my mind was having trouble taking everything in. It was like traveling to a foreign country where you knew a little of the language and you had to watch everyone's lips to make sure you followed what they were saying and you didn't make a fool of yourself. The Circle was performed Skyclad, a fancy word for naked. I was offered a ceremonial robe, which I accepted with great gusto. While everyone's own experience is unique, I can speak for mine: being Skyclad certainly brings everyone down to a common denominator, serving to put everyone on the same footing. Women and men who look glamorous in clothes are just regular folk without them. Men also seem a little more deferential when exposed this way. The biggest surprise of all was that, thinking about it afterward, my own body didn't seem nearly so hideous to me. During part of the ritual, the Priestess said that each of us was made in the image of the Goddess and that each of us was Her perfect child. A lot of Catholic-induced, uncomfortable shame seemed to seep out of me. Afterward, I was able to walk through my own house naked for the first time (my husband hadn't even considered this fringe benefit). I was also able to participate in the next Circle Skyclad; the experience opened my eyes to the beauty of every woman and man, including my own.

Does that last sentence sound rather self-absorbed? Amazingly, most Pagan faiths allow, even encourage, taking care of yourself and loved ones, physically, mentally, and spiritually, inside and out. No one is asked to suffer or sacrifice for some mystical reward at the end of life. Taking control of your own life, empowering yourself to say, "I deserve *more* than mere survival, and if the world thinks my body needs fixing, they're the ones who miss out on the beauty and freedom of life."

These teachers and their local students hosted a series of public concerts, seminars, and lectures on Wicca and related topics, such as drumming and chanting, women's and men's mysteries as practiced in traditional faiths, folk music, and others. There were some forty people at the drumming and chanting seminar. Lots of couples, a few gay, most straight, most European-Americans, some Native Americans, one African-American woman. We sat on the floor in an oblong Circle which wrapped itself around bookcases (the meeting was held in a women's bookstore) and did different exercises with noise makers and with our voices, all of them designed to introduce us to one another or to focus on things we wanted in our lives. It was surprising to me how much you learned about the individuals in the group in just a few hours of playing.

After the seminar was over, people were excitedly exchanging phone numbers and talking about getting together; I was not convinced this was such a good idea. These people *seemed* nice, but did I trust them? What was I getting into?

The proprietor of the bookstore, who served as a resource for all women in the community, began facilitating a network of Pagans who came to the various seminars and customers who approached her about a Coven. Finally, in February of 1991, the bookshelves were pushed back out of the way, a green tarp was taped across the storefront, and seven strangers talked nervously. After some brief, first-name-only introductions, our odd assortment of women sat down in a semicircle facing Laurel, the brave woman who had called the meeting. She was the impetus behind the group; she had researched everything that she was going to say and the way the altar was to be set up.

The women at that meeting were all pretty mainstream—one was president of a local women's organization; one was a lawyer in a prominent firm; one was a freelance writer; and one attended church with my family every week (although she didn't know us personally). And now, all these women considered *me* a Wiccan, one affiliated with a national Coven. This gave me pause for thought, like waking up at work and realizing you still have on your pajamas. What was I doing? Did I really want people to know I was a Witch?

Even with the tension I felt, there was a different kind of excitement and anticipation with this group of women than I had had with other groups. These were really *my* kind of people, if there was such a thing, and they were all interested in the same things that had led me to meeting with Pagans in the first place. It would be much later that I learned that a good number of us were from alcoholic or otherwise dysfunctional homes; most of us were overachievers with an incredible sense of responsibility and loyalty; all of us were looking for affirmation of our gender and beliefs.

Over the year-and-a-day, there were as many as thirty people at a Circle and as few as five. Sometimes I knew everyone there, but at the larger meetings I often met people I can't even remember now. There were meetings at the bookstore, there were meetings on farmland, there were meetings at lake resorts and rented cabins in the woods; there were meetings in living rooms and in backyards. There were just fun meetings and rented movies; there were times of sorrow and grief and pain in each of our lives and in the life of the Circle. Of the seven of us there at the first meeting, there were four in the group who eventually took Covenstead. We have celebrated the births and deaths and unions and dissolutions in each other's lives. We have blessed each other's new dwellings, and cried together when violence touched our families. We have learned from one another and shared our knowledge. We have each grown in subtle and not so subtle ways. Each new face over the year gave the Circle its own gentle light, and the strands of the web were woven tightly. Where there have been breaks, time and love and trust have patched the rents. The thirteen Women of my Circle are connected to me and I see the magic of living each day more intensely because of them.

During the course of my first year in the Coven, I attended two Catholic funerals. Both were for relatives and, although I felt close to my family, I felt more like an observer at the Requiem Mass. The striking similarity in what the priests did and what we do in the Circle hit me like a ton of bricks. In all those years in catechism we were taught that priests were the only ones who could celebrate the mass the way God wanted it to be done, and that not even a nun could speak to God directly, because she was a woman. During the funeral the priest walked with incense around the casket widdershins: this is the same way Pagans open a Circle. This may be just a coincidence, or it may be just another of the old traditions that Catholicism adopted from the older religions. Either way, I know that I am truly entitled to create ritual for myself. I am Priestess, and so are all women.

The strength and love in our Coven has filled the gaps in my life quite nicely, thank you. I am empowered to be whole, to be free, to be wild if I want or to rock a baby gently if I feel like it; to love myself, to love other people unconditionally. The evolution of the recovery begun for me in a 12-Step program has brought me here: I am Witch, I am Wise Woman, I am the Goddess' Perfect Child, I am Loved, I am Free.

Blessed Be.

COVEN MANAGEMENT BY CONSENSUS

FROM THE very beginning, the women of Copper Key set about establishing and revising the ways in which the group handled conflict, resolved minor and major crises, planned events, and determined the course of the group. Even down to deciding when they would meet and who would serve as Priestess, the group as a whole had a hand in making the decisions. At first, voting on these issues was not a matter of how long you had been a member or whether or not you had attended enough meetings; rather, if you were there and there was an issue on the table, you were asked to help make the decision.

Determining which matters needed to be resolved was a little murkier; after all, if you hadn't been studying the Craft for any length of time, how would you know what a Circle was supposed to do?

Leadership

"I think it's normal group dynamics for there to always be a leader bee and follower bees, and I think it was a natural situation when this group first started, idiotic as it may sound, that everyone looked to me for direction even though I didn't have a clue what to do next," Laurel said. "I had no more experience in Wicca than anyone in there, even less than some. But I think the important thing is that as quickly as that person can, she should relinquish that authority to the group."

Early on, Laurel paved the way for the Circle to develop its own traditions by making it clear that whoever served as Priestess would determine the type of ritual that would be celebrated. Her eclectic first meeting gave way to a standard Hidden Grove Sabbat led by Acacia, shortly followed by Tara's purely Dianic Full Moon. Some early meetings had a more Native American flavor. This type of experimentation prepared the members of the group to choose the path which they would follow together. After all, many of the women had never experienced any type of alternative spirituality firsthand, and their safety inside Copper Key allowed them the flexibility they needed to make their own decisions on religion, spirituality, and ways of life.

Some of the first decisions made by the Circle include the following.

Male Membership
At the very beginning, a concerted effort was made to discover men who might be interested in working with Copper Key. Eventually, only Laurel's husband Seal was identified as a potential member. Rather than put undue pressure on him or on the other members, it was decided that Moon meetings would be open to women only, and that Sabbats would be open to guests of both genders. Because of his interest in Wicca and his relationship with Laurel, Seal often served as Priest at the Sabbats where significant others were invited to attend.

Open and Closed Meetings
By July of the first year, the group realized that the constant influx of new members and visitors made bonding as a group more difficult and also decreased working energy the Circle would need to function as a Coven. However, they also realized that without new members the group might stagnate or even die off due to attrition. Their compromise: New Moons, which had been identified as teaching meetings, would be open to newcomers and visitors; Full Moons would be closed to anyone who had not yet attended a meeting of Copper Key.

The decision for open/closed meetings necessitated defining membership and providing a way to bring in new members. Rather than set a limit on the number of women who could belong, Copper Key left recruitment to the Gods and focused their attention on administering the process by which new members could be brought in. After quite a bit of debate, the women determined that potential members would be required to attend at least two New Moons before they would be invited to attend a Full Moon, and that they would be required to attend at least one Full Moon before being invited to a Sabbat.

Meeting the Public

Copper Key also came to the conclusion that the best way to screen visitors or potential new members was to have someone from the group meet them in public for lunch or dinner or tea before they would be invited to their first New Moon.

Ritual Attire

In the Coven's first two years, Skyclad was not an option discussed with any sincerity. However, the group did vote to wear robes at their closed meetings to take them completely out of the mundane. No specific pattern or color or material was chosen. The women selected colors and decorations that suited their personalities and which had personal meaning for them. One seamstress was hired by six of the women to sew robes—they told her they all belonged to the same alumnae organization of a collegiate sorority.

Parliamentary Procedure

While it may seem out of place in a religious meeting, a loosely-defined Robert's Rules was adopted, whereby motions were made and seconded, debate for and against was aired, and the vote was called and cast on all decisions. Due notice was given; issues to be voted upon were announced at two consecutive meetings, and the votes were cast at the third. Eventually, the votes occurred only at Full Moons when visitors were no longer included in the process.

Conflict Within the Coven

Later in the evolution of Copper Key, the women defined ways to handle conflict within the Circle and ways of allowing members to move on (some of these will be discussed in Chapter VII).

"I think Covens are like shooting stars: they take off across the night sky in a big roar of light and fury, and they eventually burn out," Laurel said. "I think the ones that go on and on and on are really to be commended, because obviously they have figured out something in self-government that works."

FINDING A TEACHER

THE WOMEN of Copper Key are very opinionated on the topic of whether or not finding a teacher is essential to learning the Craft. They do not even agree with each other. Here's an excerpt of one of their debates on the subject:

Ginger: By going to a teacher, you pick up a mind set that says, "I don't know," and the problem that this creates in Wicca is that you do know, you already know everything.

River: But a good teacher doesn't tell you what they think, they lead you to what you think.

Ginger: You already have a good teacher, and the only good teacher is yourself. Anyone else is just a mirror to look into, and you have to understand that there are ripples in that mirror, and what you see is not necessarily what is really true. The problem with mentors is that they just move you through the track faster. You're going to learn how to say the words and do the ritual faster with someone telling you how. You won't understand it, and it won't have meaning, but—

River: If they are a good mentor, you will.

Ginger: I've never seen a good one then.

River: I understand that you've had problems with the way Hidden Grove[1] taught, but you can't tell me you've never been led to any sort of knowledge by another person. A good teacher should be able to bring questions to your mind that you've never considered before.

Orchid: I've read that you cannot teach someone else. They must absolutely come to their own conclusions through their own experiences, by their own initiative, and there is just no other way.

Foxfire: You pass on knowledge, you don't teach *why* to ritual.

Mer-Nuit: I think that Hidden Grove taught us a lot. We used their teaching tapes a great deal, but those tapes said, "In our tradition, this is the only way." And we rejected that part.

Ginger: I don't know that there's any way to teach what Wicca is —it is essentially an experiential, mystic phenomenon. Given the essence of that, when you enter into a relationship where one person says, "I know and you don't," that person has power over rather than a relationship.

Mer-Nuit: I think you have a problem with power over.

River: Okay, I have friends who want to learn about the Craft. They really don't know where to start. It's not that they don't think they have knowledge already there in their own minds, it's just that they don't know where to start. And I'll say, "Well, go to the park, sit down by a stream, and think about what it means to you." Some people would call that teaching, or leading them to where they can teach themselves. Some people need other people's help to find their own way.

Ginger: When I want to learn mathematics, I'll take a course. And for a certain kind of learning, for a limited curriculum, that

---

[1] A teaching Coven with which many members of Copper Key were at one time affiliated.

might work just fine. But in Wicca, if you go into it assuming you know nothing, you've missed the essence. If the essence is, "I'm the Goddess' perfect child," then who is going to be your teacher?

Foxfire: I think you're talking about two different things. There's a level of basic knowledge, and then there is personal experience.

River: Okay, so a Teacher cannot teach you the Craft, or give you a spiritual life. But suppose you want to be closer to the Moon, a teacher can't tell you how to be closer to the Moon, but a teacher can give you some experiences to try that will let you feel that way. A teacher is there to show you the signposts along the way.

Mer-Nuit: We've all come to points in the Craft where we've needed to ask someone, "What's happening here?" or "What's this all about?"

River: Exactly. I could be starting out in the Craft all by myself and sit and meditate and start hearing voices, and I could think I was totally crazy.

Mer-Nuit: And that'd be the typical reaction.

Ginger: There is a real difference between that kind of response to a phenomenon and teaching. When I first got to know Orchid, she told me about doing her self-dedication, that afterward she was so exhausted she fell down. I told her that it sounded like what we do and that she might try eating a little something afterward. I was in no way teaching her anything.

River: That's exactly what you were doing. You and I must be talking about two entirely different things—you mean someone who lectures, and I mean someone who gives you advice, who helps you answer questions for yourself, someone who has more experience.

Acacia: Where did you learn what you told Orchid to do?

Ginger: That's what I heard from Hidden Grove. Here's the difference in the way I got it and the way I passed it on: first, I was told that only the High Priestess ever drew down,[2] and when she did it was very dangerous and we shouldn't try it. That was clearly establishing a power over hierarchy.

River: But I've seen people who weren't ready try it, and they've wigged out completely. That's legitimate advice that they gave you.

Ginger: I've never seen anybody go nuts. But that information was given to me in a context where I hadn't even asked. When Orchid asked me, I had extreme reverence not only for the experience that had happened to her, but for the fact that she had experienced this for herself. I don't think it would have happened to someone who was not an extraordinary woman. The only thing I could say to her was a tiny gift of appreciation. I had to tell her that maybe a piece of bread when she does this would help because she was very powerful. It was like entering into something that I was privileged to share with her. I think that's what happens in Copper Key.

Mer-Nuit: There is nothing wrong with having a teacher. I don't see what this whole discussion is about.

River: I've learned a lot from Acacia, I've learned a lot from Ginger, I've learned a lot from everyone in Copper Key, and I hope that you have all learned something from me. I consider us all teachers, but I don't think I'm any higher or lower than you, that you are more spiritual than I or vice versa.

Mer-Nuit: We do teach each other.

---

[2] Took the energy of the Goddess or God within her/himself.

River: We need a word for that, for a non-hierarchical teaching situation.

Ginger: I think that what goes on in here is a kind of sharing. Everyone here is at some point nurtured, and everyone here is at some point a nurturer.

River: Have you ever heard the expression, "the best teachers learn from their students"? Whenever you explain some concept to another person, you often end up understanding it better yourself.

It would seem that each member of Copper Key does indeed share her knowledge and personal experience with other members of her Coven. Entering into a formal arrangement to study with a person or a group, even on a national level, should be considered cautiously. Most people who advertise in publications to teach students for a fee are running a scam; if any potential teacher asks you for money, it should be considered a red flag. Occasionally, you may reimburse a teacher for the costs of printed materials, or for the cost of renting a room for the class, but by and large, if someone asks for an exorbitant amount of money, watch out.

"There are some people who claim to be teachers and use that power to convince people to do things that they are not comfortable with," Tara said. "The Craft is such a hidden subject, that if I tell you I am the only way that you can ever be initiated as a Witch, and the first thing you have to do is sleep with me or give me $500, and you really want to be a part of a Coven, you might just do it. I wish I could say that it doesn't happen in the Craft, but the sad thing is that it happens everywhere."

When first interested in studying the Craft, people often feel unable to fully come into their own in the religion without finding a teacher. "For a long time I thought that to have any validity whatsoever, I was just going to have to have a teacher; I couldn't possibly figure this all out for myself, and if I did, I wouldn't know that I had because there'd be nobody to tell me that I had finally got it," Laurel said. "How would anyone else ever believe me, because I wouldn't have any degree. So I fell in with a teacher who was at that time working on a national level. My relationship with her was different from her relationship with a lot of other people because I was older than she and I was not 'blinded by the light.' She was always surrounded by so many sycophants. I really can't say that she taught me anything that I couldn't have gotten from a book, though she gave me a lot of useful technical knowledge. My favorite way to conduct a Circle is still basically her way, because it is so familiar to me, and I am very comfortable with the symbolism. But the insights that I've had that have really made a difference in my spiritual development have not been at Circles that her group conducted, even when there was a drawing down, but rather things I learned on my own or in Copper Key, where no one professes to be a teacher."

Acacia expressed an even stronger opinion on the teaching that she received while studying with Hidden Grove: "Mer-Nuit got her hands on a copy of Aidan Kelly's book about Gardnerian Craft. None of us had ever claimed to be Gardnerian; in fact, I had never even picked up a book on the Gardnerian system because most of us had heard a lot about the sex magick and scourging and basically thought it sounded like a dirty old man's religion. I was horrified when she showed me Kelly's book—ritual we had been practicing for over a year as students, things we had been told were Fam Trad, were written there almost word for word, including a lot of the prayers and invocations. I was furious with myself for not finding out sooner."

Laurel added, "Trust your own instincts. Witches are born, not made. You can't teach somebody how to be a Witch; you can make it easier for them by showing them a way to find some answers, but the truth of the matter is that if this is your path and you are seeking the Goddess, you will find Her whether you have a teacher, whether you're doing it alone or in a group, just trust your own instincts. If something feels spiritually balanced to you, it is something that you should be doing."

If you feel that a teacher is the best way for you to learn the Craft, you might try these ways to find one.

- Write to the authors of your favorite books on the subject and find out what their policies are for accepting students.
- Attend a Pagan Gathering where many Craft personalities are scheduled to speak.

- Ask your local contacts: bookstore owners, friends, Circle members, retreat centers, etc.
- Look for a Pagan Student Alliance on the local college campus.
- Subscribe to various Pagan newsletters and contact those that seem to be in line with your own opinions (see Appendix 2 for some suggestions).
- Check to see if the Unitarian Universalist Church in your area has a CUUPS (Covenant of Unitarian Universalist Pagans) chapter. See about joining the group or ask for a schedule of events—a CUUPS chapter can be an excellent networking resource.

Once you have found a potential teacher, do not be afraid to interview that person or group—you are, after all, planning to invest a considerable amount of time, and you will also be opening yourself up to scrutiny. Never feel that because you are new to the situation you must submit wholly to their way of thinking, doing things, or behaving. While many rituals, particularly those of initiation, contain elements designed to take one by surprise, in the beginning you should never do anything with which you are uncomfortable. "Perfect love and perfect trust" are *earned* both by the group and by the individual.

JOURNAL ENTRIES

1. Acacia's story brought to mind these things:

2. How do I feel about learning the Craft from books? from a teacher? from a group or Circle? Which method might I respond to best?

3. If I were in a Coven, how would I prefer that it be governed? Would I be more comfortable having a hand in leading a group, or would I prefer a strong High Priestess or Priest to make decisions for the group?

4. These are the things I feel I should know before agreeing to study with any teacher:

5. What role do I normally play in organizations to which I belong?

COPPER KEY RECOMMENDS:

Witch Amongst Us: The Autobiography of a Witch, by Lois Bourne; London: Robert Hale Limited, © 1985.

4
CELEBRATIONS

ORCHID'S STORY

"YOU'RE NEVER gonna believe what I'm reading," I say over the phone to my best friend who lives two states away, "The *Witches Bible, Compleat*." Now this friend of mine has always been the kind you could tell anything to without judgment. We met at a NOW meeting and were attracted to each other immediately, discovering that our experiences and philosophies about life were very similar. However, I didn't know exactly what to expect. Would she hang up in horror? Laugh as if it were a joke? I had a contingency plan for every response except the one I got.

"I don't believe it!" she exclaimed. "When you called, I was reading *Ariadne's Thread*. I've dropped out of NOW and am involved with a group who practices Wicca. Isn't it wonderful?" Then followed a two-hour discussion of modern American Wicca and how we both found that it empowered us as women and enriched our lives spiritually.

This was just the first of numerous other instances which proved to me that Wicca is quite a large movement with women today. For instance, at dinner I overhear the group at the next table talking about modern-day Witches; sitting on my back porch I overhear my next-door neighbors talking about their woman friend who is into "feminist theology"; at work a client mentions that one of the reasons he got a divorce was his lack of understanding of his wife's new interest in "Earth-based spirituality." I recently read some statistics that show that Paganism is the fastest-growing religion today—outpacing even Christian fundamentalism.

But getting to the point where I could actually tell someone I was a Witch (coming "out of the broom closet") was a long process and

I feel I should share that journey. Raised in the finest Southern Baptist tradition, I grew to hate the hypocrisy and misogyny of the Bible. I was horrified at what atrocities had been justified in the name of God and other deities throughout history, so I totally rejected any kind of spirituality because it all seemed to be organized and spread with always the same effects: suppression of diversity and domination of many by a few. However, I still clung, albeit tenuously, to the concept of the interconnectedness of all things living. It would take years for this single thought to congeal into a whole philosophy.

Having renounced Christianity, I found there were few places to go for a spiritual community in my home town (a medium-sized, conservative city in Louisiana). However, over a period of about six years I became friends with several people who attended the Unitarian Church. The Unitarians make a genuine effort to see diversity as a strength, valuing each individual's spiritual path as divine in its own right. It was through the Unitarian belief of tolerance and the living example I saw in my friends (one an atheist, one gay, two Christians, two Humanists) that I overcame my fears that religion was nothing more than conformity and mind control.

Although I never joined the Unitarian Church, I am grateful that it was through their "Cakes for the Queen of Heaven" course in feminist theology that I discovered Witchcraft. As I began to read the chapter on the reemergence of Witchcraft, I was shocked, amazed and elated to find that my personal beliefs were being itemized right before my eyes! Shocked because these beliefs were once the primary religion in ancient times; elated because there were others living today with the same beliefs. Months later looking back at this chapter in the study book, I saw that I had penned these words at the bottom of the very last page: "I AM A WITCH!"

That took some getting used to, I must say. Three centuries of Christian propaganda have twisted our society's image of Witches. What used to be a revered position in ancient communities (the healers, the old wise women) is now portrayed as a green-skinned, wart-nosed, child-eating hag. Did you know that nine million people were tortured to death during the years of the Inquisition, Christianity's last effort to stomp out Goddess worship? The majority of these were single women, women property owners, women midwives and healers. Besides the horrors of the women's own suffering, their children were made to testify against them and were forced to watch them die. Yes, women had a Holocaust.

Now, as then, the men in control don't relish the thought of women coming into their own power. Taking away their male God shakes the foundations of the patriarchical system that gives them so much privilege: privilege to rape and incest women, privilege to war and kill, privilege to pollute the Earth. Witchcraft and its reverence for all life and the Earth stand in direct contrast to these things. If you love the Earth as your Mother, you can't pollute her; if you live as if you have only power within yourself (not power over other people) there would never be wars or oppression. If the feminine were divine, rape and incest could not exist. The principles of Witchcraft and Goddess worship are beautiful but threatening to traditional male-dominated religions.

However, despite the female basis of Wicca, there are men who are moved enough by its principles to call themselves Pagans. (My Coven is all female by choice. I have met only three men who were interested, but then only one was a serious practitioner). What happens when you are already married and discover that you are a Witch? This is precisely my predicament. Usually, my husband is a liberal person who believes in tolerance to a fault and actually stood up in front of a large gathering of his peers and made a public appeal for the acceptance of Wicca. But he is having more trouble on a personal level with my involvement.

As I found out the history behind the Craft and what it is really all about, I began to long to find a group of women who call themselves Witches with pride. It wasn't long before I had two books that I used as guidelines.

My first ritual was a self-dedication. I bathed and sat naked before my altar. I always perform my at-home rituals Skyclad because it seems to help you leave the trappings of this world behind (I have never personally attended a group gathering where everyone was Skyclad). I am still amazed at the power of this first ritual. Without realizing it at the time, as I called in the Directions and called upon the Goddess, my head became heavy and I grew warm all over. At the closing of the ritual, I bade the Directions farewell, thanked the

Goddess for her presence, and as I blew out the candle I felt a sort of a "swoosh" from deep within me. Then, all of a sudden I felt cold and very aware of my nudity. I immediately climbed into bed and fell into a deep sleep.

I woke up the next day really refreshed and definitely feeling somehow different about myself. I believe that I 'drew down' the power of the Goddess into myself that night (or up from within myself) and I believe it so strongly that sometimes I wonder if people can somehow tell that I'm a Witch now just by looking. I have been told that such an inexperienced Witch as myself accomplished an impressive feat because usually students of Wicca learn this 'drawing down' skill at a much later stage.

It was at this first ritual that I asked for guidance on my new Wiccan path, and I believe that it was in response to this request that just three months later I was asked to join a Coven! I had met a couple of times with one member of the Coven, whose name was given to me by the owner of a bookstore that sells women's spirituality books. Here was just what I had been looking for, but I was scared to death at first. I had never even met any of the other members of the Coven. It was a closed group and because of their secrecy they would only let you meet with them if you were deemed to be serious about your Wiccan path and mature enough not to do anything to damage the reputations of any of the members. They had had one bad experience with someone who was not discreet and so they reluctantly made this rule.

Would I join the Coven? What would my non-Pagan friends say? What if my ex-husband found out? Would he try to take custody of my child away? Should I raise my child Wiccan? I worked for an attorney whom I could never tell. Would these people have purple hair and rings through their noses? Would I like them? A thousand questions ran through my head but still the Witch in me said, "YES." This wise woman has not led me down the wrong path yet! And what a wonderful array of women they are: ages twenty to fifty, every profession, every size, every shape. They are actually so average that it makes me laugh when I think back on my first fears about joining.

The Coven meets every Full Moon, every Sabbat, and some of us meet New Moons, too. It is hard to find adequate words to express my appreciation of the nurturing I get from my sister Witches and my indebtedness to Witchcraft for helping me reclaim my femininity. You see, I had always been an ardent feminist but somewhere deep in me my Southern Baptist upbringing still reigned. On a deep spiritual level I still believed in the inherent inferiority of the female. NEVER AGAIN. If there were some spell I could use to empower every woman on this planet with the teachings of Witchcraft, I would cast it in a minute.

Pure Witchcraft doesn't knock at your door like the Jehovah's Witnesses. Its voice rises up from deep within your being. The voice has been there for 5,000 years and some women aren't able to hear it anymore because they have been conditioned to focus outward to other people's needs and the works that men have created. A song by the Indigo Girls goes, "Well, darkness has a hunger that's insatiable, and lightness has a call that's hard to hear..."[1] It's hard to hear, but more and more women are turning inward and listening, listening.

I have been a member of the Coven for seven months now. I am reading whatever I can to learn more about the Craft, but experience is the best teacher. That's one of the reasons our Coven has no hierarchy. The other reason is that Witchcraft is naturally non-hierarchical. No one thing is better than another; all are interdependent and have a special purpose and place on the spiral of life. Therefore, we have no single High Priestess. Each woman decides when she will lead a ritual and what will take place at that particular ritual. We generally pattern the Sabbats after traditional rituals, but our Moons are our own creations, meeting the needs of the Coven members or just celebrating the appropriate aspect of the Wheel of the Year.

I have found that I have become more aware of the phases of the Moon, of my menstrual cycles, of the cycles of the Seasons. I have become more calm and accepting of the flow of life instead of always fighting against it. And unlike any religion I know of, Wicca does not run away from death. Wicca knows that Death is the greatest gift of the Goddess. Think about it. If we lived forever, what would matter? Why smell roses, we would have an eternity to do it. Why savor the

---

[1] The Indigo Girls, CLOSER TO FINE, © 1989, CBS Records, Inc.

beauty of a warm summer morning, we would have an eternity to enjoy it. Why have children to love, nurture, and play with, we would live forever... Nothing makes life so sweet as death. And if you know that your reward for living lies not in some place in the sky called heaven but in the living itself, you can relax and more fully enjoy and appreciate everything around you.

I love the fact that Wicca does not blame or place fault—it assigns responsibility. There is a distinction made between something that you have done wrong either through uninformed or hasty decisions and something from outside of you that happens such as a thief stealing your car. You are responsible for your actions, which implies authority and power, even the power to learn from mistakes. Fault and blame (such as the Protestant concept of sin) imply guilt and keep you powerless.

But the thing I love most about Wicca is the tenet that simply to be is divine and justification enough for existence. There is no need to search for a deity to follow. You, yourself, are an aspect of the holy and therefore sacred. And should act accordingly. There is no searching to be done, all the power you ever need is within your reach — it's inside you. To put it another way: "I have been with you from the beginning and I am that which is attained at the end of desire."[2]

Blessed Be.

---

[2] From the Change of the Goddess–see *The Spiral Dance*, page 90, by Starhawk for her version.

ELEMENTS OF COPPER KEY
RITUAL CELEBRATIONS

The Ritual Bath

It became the habit for Copper Key to set up an area for members to go by themselves for a few minutes to prepare for the ritual. Some sources recommend a full bath in a tub for each member; Copper Key adapted this practice into what came to be known as The Ritual Bird Bath. Normally, a bathroom sink was filled with warm water, to which was added a small amount of salt and flower petals or herbs, depending on the occasion and the tastes of the member setting it up. Candles were usually placed around the sink on the counter, and incense was lit and left burning while members took their turn. Using the bathroom sink versus a bowl of water in the ritual space means being able to shut the door and spend some time alone and also have a mirror over the water, often an aid in focusing.

Each person decides the best way to achieve a relaxed state once they are in the bath—either a self-anointing, or deep breathing, or a mirror exercise, or opening the chakras, or splashing around—whatever the Coven member's personal choice may be. The simple self-blessing which follows is adapted from many different sources.

- Stand facing the mirror above the basin with both feet flat on the ground, about 12 inches apart (you should feel comfortable and balanced).
- Stretch your neck gently or roll your shoulders to release tension.
- Dip your fingertips into the warm water and use that hand to touch

- the top of your head; say, "Bless me, Lord & Lady, for I am your child."

- the center of your forehead; say, "Bless my mind, that it be open."

- your lips; say, "Bless my lips, that I may speak Your words."

- your heart; say, "Bless my heart, that I may love unconditionally."

- your womb/groin; say, "Bless my womb/groin, that I may be inspired in all acts of creativity."

- your knees; say, "Bless my knees, that I may kneel in holy places."

- the top of your feet; say, "Bless my feet, that I may walk Your path."

- the top of your head; say, "Bless me, Lord & Lady, for I am your child."

The basin can be elaborately decorated with shells, stones, flowers, plants, images of the Gods, pictures, special items, or can be very simple with just a candle on the counter near the basin. One or two members of the group should volunteer or be assigned well in advance of the meeting time to set up the space. No matter how simple or elaborate the space, the Ritual Bath is an important step to preparing mentally for Circle.

If your group uses the Bath, allow at least three to five minutes per person; this can add a considerable amount of time to the meeting. If there is a time problem for any member of your group, you may want to set up two areas for this purpose. If all else fails, and you know that you will run into a problem by taking the time, this procedure can be skipped. All tools and procedures used in the ritual process are there to help the Coven focus their minds and attention on the celebration at hand, and can be chosen by the group or the Priestess for the evening.

Attire

While some groups choose to practice Skyclad (ritually nude), Copper Key chose to design special robes for closed meetings. For open meetings, the only requirements are that clothes be clean, no shoes be worn inside the ritual space, all jewelry worn be consecrated and have special meaning to the wearer, and no watches be worn.

Challenge

One tradition, said to have been handed down from the Burning Times, is the Challenge. This involves stopping each person as they approach to enter the Circle and asking them for a password or some sign that they belong to the Circle or Coven. Most sources say that this was to protect the Coveners from spies who might reveal the identities of those in attendance and have them arrested, or worse.

In order to do the Challenge, your group should decide upon some phrase or word or even a secret handshake. Of course, there should not be anyone present whom someone in the group has not invited in the first place. If you choose to omit the Challenge, it is okay. Anyone who has been Challenged, however, knows that it is an experience a person won't soon forget! As it has been handed down in many different traditions, Copper Key chose to use this practice only at large Circles when guests were present and at Circles when new members were being brought in.

One woman is selected by the Priestess to carry out the Challenge. The Challenger stands with her back to the ritual space and holds a staff to bar the way of each person who approaches the altar until she gives the appropriate signal. When a guest cannot provide this sign, the Challenger turns to the Circle, and says, "(Name) has come and does not have a password. Will anyone speak for (Name)?" Someone already seated then responds, "Yes, I know (Name) and will speak for her/him."

It is easier to carry out the Challenge as each person emerges from the Ritual Bath and approaches the Circle. When using the Challenge, Coven members should go into the bath ahead of the guests and newcomers.

After each person has been in the Bath and has been Challenged, she should take a seat around the Altar, as directed by the Priestess, and remain quiet until the ritual begins.

Meditation

A group meditation at the opening of a ritual further helps the group get grounded and helps them synchronize their thoughts and intent. When the group is focusing on the same ideas or objects, it is getting tuned up to work together during the ritual.

Sweeping

This task is usually reserved for the Handmaiden or youngest female member of the Coven; the Priestess may, however, assign this to any member present. Starting in the East and proceeding clockwise, the Handmaiden sweeps around everyone at the altar, both physically and mentally removing any dirt or negative feelings away from the Circle. The Broom, called a Besom, is left in the East propped bristles up.

Mer-Nuit wrote the following sweeping meditation for a Full Moon Ceremony:

Tonight I want to begin with the sweeping...
We sweep the Circle in preparation
Using a woman's tool to create our sacred space
Using a woman's tool to make ready
As the ancient midwife makes ready the birthing room,
          sweeping away malicious & evil spirits.
As the good mother makes the house ready on Solstice eve,
          sweeping to welcome good & helpful spirits.
We sweep because the door will be opened...
We sweep because the veil will be parted...
We sweep to make ready the sacred Circle.

May all evil run out,
May all good run in.

Ritual Tools

Copper Key chose to use ritual tools during almost all of its formal meetings. The tools referred to in the scripts that follow are used by Copper Key, but each group may have its own ideas about what magical implements it would like to employ; it is a good idea to remember that the traditions of Wicca are homemade—members often use items normally found around the house rather than specialized ritual equipment, i.e., a simple carving knife from the kitchen for the Athame, the broom that always sat by the hearth for Sweeping, a little cinnamon from the cabinet for incense. Whatever you feel most comfortable with is best.

The following are the tools which will be referred to in the ritual scripts that follow:

Candles:	*Source/Union Candle*–normally the tallest point on the altar
	Goddess & God Candles–one for each
	South Candle–a red candle to represent Fire
	Utility taper–on the altar to light other candles
	Snuffer–helpful but not mandatory
Broom:	A utilitarian or special ritual broom
Staff:	Generally a tall, thick walking stick
Wand:	The personal tool of the Priestess; generally wooden.
Athame:	Ritual knife, usually the personal tool of the Priestess
Incense:	Cone, stick, or powdered incense and an appropriate holder
Bell:	Any type
Chalice:	A goblet or special cup to hold the Wine
Plate:	To hold Cakes
Three Bowls:	One to hold Water
	One to hold Salt
	One for Libations–the first cake, the first bit of wine, and the first portions of each dish of the Feast

Casting the Circle

The Circle is cast to create a space in which to worship. It is outside of time and the mundane world. Everyone stands and faces the altar;

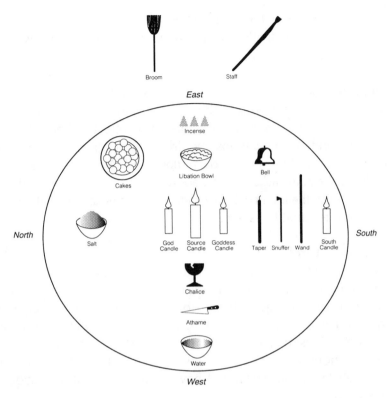

Arrange the tools on the Altar (which may be a raised platform, table, or area on the floor) as diagramed above.

the Priestess takes the Wand and walks clockwise to the East. From that point, she walks around the circle three times deosil (*with the sun, clockwise*). The Priestess may choose to explain the use of the Circle to the group as she does this or write a meditation to share while she treads.

Calling the Quarters
Wiccans generally believe in the existence of the Elemental Spirits of each direction, and these spirits are given respect and reverence. For each ritual celebration, these Spirits or "Watchtowers" are invited to witness the rites of the group. They are called in before the Gods and asked to return to their usual realms after the Gods have departed. The

Moon and Sabbat rituals in the next two sections will provide you with invocations and meditations on each Direction, or you may wish to write your own.

Inviting the Gods
After the Circle has been cast, the Priestess and Priest (or Priestesses) invite the Goddess and the God to enter the Circle, to witness the rites to be celebrated. Invocations should be appropriate to the Deity invoked. The Goddess and God candles should be lit from the Union candle as they are asked in. As soon as this is accomplished, the Priestess states the intent of the Circle, i.e., to celebrate the Full Moon, to consecrate ritual tools, etc.

Work of the Circle
This is the point in any ritual celebration when focused energy is used to effect an outcome: spells. Rather than turning lumps of lead into gold or cursing bosses with hair loss, Wiccan spells are generally concerned with self-improvement, healing, environmental repair, world consciousness, and global harmony. The Wiccan Rede, "And you harm none, do as you will," and the law of three (that whatever you do returns to you three times), governs all respectable practitioners of the Craft.

Each Sabbat generally has a traditional spell that the Coven may wish to include at this time, usually concerned with the time of the year and the progression of the Wheel. Members of the Circle may bring their own spells as well, having discussed them with the Priestess prior to the start of the ritual. Whatever their concern, most sources say that each ritual should be limited to three magical works.

Wine & Cakes
One of the most important elements of any ritual is the blessing and sharing of Wine & Cakes. Eating and drinking grounds a person and brings her back down to Earth after a spiritual experience. If anyone in the Circle feels lightheaded or is uncomfortable with the way she feels during a ritual, she should eat a bit of cake from the altar immediately and should find that the feelings soon dissipate. The

formal celebration of Wine & Cakes is also a way to thank the Gods for their bounty and ask for continued blessings.

The Chalice is usually filled with fruit juice rather than wine on Copper Key's altar, out of respect for anyone who chooses not to imbibe. Any natural drink will do; the group was even able to find pomegranate nectar and other seasonally appropriate drinks. During the re-birthing ritual at Mabon, 1991, milk was used; it was soon discovered that a particular member would no more swallow milk than drink gasoline! In the best interests of the group, whoever is responsible for bringing the Wine should check to be sure that everyone can share what is used in the Chalice.

Cakes can be store-bought or homemade, breads, cakes, or cookies, even brownies. A selection on the plate often makes the Circle run more smoothly, as some people are allergic to ingredients like nuts, chocolate, wheat, etc. Once your group has been meeting for a while, these things should be common knowledge; in the beginning, it is best to check before cooking or shopping. The recipe below is for Sophia's moon cookies, which she brought to Copper Key's first meeting:

> *1 cup ground almonds*
> *1 1/2 cups flour*
> *1/2 cup confectioner's sugar*
> *3 drops almond extract*
> *1/2 cup butter, softened*
> *1 egg yolk*

Combine almonds, flour, sugar and extract. With your hands, work in butter and egg yolk. Chill dough. Preheat oven to 325°F. Pinch off dough into golfball-sized pieces. Shape into crescents and put on greased cookie sheets. Bake 20 minutes or until light brown.

Feast

Following the ritual, it is customary to have a feast ready to be heated up for the group. Volunteers can prepare the entire meal or you can have a pot luck. It should be near the site of the altar, as the Gods are asked to stay with you until dawn for a Sabbat or Solstice celebration (*if and only if* your Coven agrees to hold vigil. If your group is unable to keep the altar set up throughout the night, then the Circle should be returned to the Earth, and the Gods and the Spirits of the Four Directions 'banished' as in the Full and New Moon Ritual prior to the Feast).

Vigil

If the Gods and the Quarters are asked to remain until morning, members of the group volunteer to take shifts with the altar throughout the night. Generally, the altar is the focal point for sitting around, telling stories, singing songs, eating, and generally being raucous. Anyone who really wants to sleep should choose a place far away! If possible, a fire nearby if not right next to the Circle is great for keeping everyone warm.

At dawn, if any of the candles are still burning, whoever is on watch should take the snuffer and reverently put out the flame. An industrious group may even want to hold a special prayer or meditation at this time. (Copper Key never got up that early as a group following a Sabbat celebration, although it was often discussed and generally considered a lovely idea.)

GINGER'S MOON MEETING

This ritual was organized and scripted by Ginger, who wishes to add "a Foreword, Disclaimers, and Assorted Notes to the Reader." Her open letter includes some advice that she and other members of the Copper Key Coven found useful in their own first Circles.

Dear Reader:

A word or two about planning ritual and scripting. The following New Moon script is based on the general outline of a Wiccan Circle. Like all effective rituals, it begins by clearing away, it creates a space, builds toward a central act or purpose, peaks, and grounds, returning the participants to a starting point. The Wiccan format is a basic structure which allows the addition of other ceremonial elements; after writing a New Moon script, adding a recitation of the Charge of the Goddess and substituting Wishes for Vows gives you a Full Moon script.

In fact, the basic New Moon script can be modified for any occasion. There is a wealth of information available on the liturgy and the theater of ritual. In the beginning, it is tempting to cut and paste rather frantically. I have found it is more effective to begin with the most important part of the ritual: the Intent. Decide what purpose the ritual should have, such as the Moon, a Sabbat, a specific event like the celebration of a new baby, a healing, or an unbinding. Once you have established what you wish to do and why, the liturgy usually falls into place. If it doesn't, perhaps you should think about the intent— is it appropriate, or is there something about it which makes you uneasy? Every Witch has good intuition and she should listen to it.

Generally, we script ritual with a combination of original work and other poems/liturgy. When possible, I recommend writing at least some original meditations or invocations. It will personalize the ritual and make it more powerful. It will also give you some guidance about the kind of spiritual work you need for personal growth. Almost from the beginning, I have felt comfortable writing elemental invocations. My association with the outdoors has always been a harmonious and magical experience. However, I find invocations for the Gods more difficult because of my rather tangled feelings about polytheism. My difficulty centers around my overall problem with understanding male energy in general. As I grow spiritually and make some progress on these issues, the ability to write invocations to Deity of both genders is improving.

There is also a strong element of performance art in Wiccan ritual, and I am very fond of it. It appeals to my inner little girl as well as the artist in me. I offer a word of caution: the *ritual* should never be the objective. It is the spiritual growth and expression that are to be nurtured. While I like a nicely structured and cohesive ritual, the mere prospect of ceremonial magic makes me exhausted. The group or Coven with which you practice will find its own level of structure and spontaneity.

On the practical side, I suggest you try any theater aspects of the ritual prior to the ritual itself. The first time I burned anything in a ritual, I used a copper-bottomed stew pot because I did not have a cauldron. The ritual was indoors and the burning paper heated the bottom of the pot so that it scorched the altar cloth and the carpet beneath it. Those three legs on a cauldron would have prevented this problem, and had I tried it in advance I would have known to call around and borrow one. Also, time is always a consideration. Rather than eliminating parts of the ritual, condense them in ways which maintain their purpose.

The New Moon script which follows is provided only as a guide; it would not win any literary awards. I hope it will provide you with a basic form and give you some confidence if you need it. Have a sense of humor. You can be serious and still not take yourself too seriously. Hear the music, join the dance, and let it rip!

Bright Blessings,
Wild Ginger

❖❖❖

Ritual Bath
Priestesses (one to sit in the East, one to sit in the West) go first.

Ground and Center
Priestess sitting in the West leads the following meditation:

"Be.

Be still.

Be aware of yourself. Feel who you are. Stretch your senses; feel where you are, touch the boundaries of your body, know the boundaries of your true self. Reach in, reach out. Open your third eye. See your true self. Know. Stretch your knowing beyond time...to the time before...the time to come...the essence of time now.

Be aware of energy...of spirit. Be aware of your fire, your flame within. See the electric spark within each nerve cell as it pulses and jumps from synapse to synapse. Be aware of the combustion of each cell as food burns to release the energy that creates us. Let your fire become one with the candle flame, the bonfire, the hearth fire, lightning, starlight, sunshine, moon beam. . . one with the spirit that encircles the universe and entwines our hearts.

Let us begin."

Sweeping
Cleansing
The incense or sage stick is passed as the Priestess says, "Smell the sweetness of Air and feel the warmth of Fire." Each person passes the incense around her space in the Circle and may fan the incense with her hand three times to her face.

Asperges
The Priestess takes the Athame and splashes a few drops of water out of the dish as she says, "This water is a symbol of the power of transformation and change. As we cast from this water, we cast also from ourselves fear, resentment, and envy."

She takes the Salt from the North and adds a few grains to the water, saying, "Salt is a symbol of Earth, of purification, and renewal.

As salt joins to water, as spirit binds to flesh, as lover enfolds the beloved, so we are all joined to the universe."

The Priestess lifts the bowl of salt water above her head in memory of every Witch who has ever mixed Salt and Water. She lowers the bowl as she says, "Let the living water of the Mother's womb purify and renew us and this place where we gather." The bowl is passed and each person sprinkles the saltwater around her spot in the Circle. If the Ritual Bath has been omitted, it is now appropriate that each member do a self-blessing, beginning with the Priestess, as well as bless each space. Touching her fingers into the water and then touching the corresponding area of the body, each member says:

> *"Bless my feet, to find true paths,*
> *Bless my knees, to kneel in holy places.*
> *Bless my womb, the portal of joy and creativity.*
> *Bless my breasts formed in beauty.*
> *Bless my lips to sing praise.*
> *Bless my eye to see the unseen.*
> *Bless my spirit, to be whole.*
> *Blessed Be."*

Men may substitute, "Bless my seed, to be sown in joy and love." The "eye" refers to the Third Eye, or psychic eye, which lies just above the nose in the center of the forehead (over the pineal gland). When all are done and the bowl returns to the Priestess in the West, she says, "We are one. Blessed Be."

Casting the Circle

All are still standing around the Circle. The Priestess now takes the hand of the woman to her left and says, "From Hand to Hand the Circle is cast." Each person in turn from the Priestess takes the hand of the person to their left and repeats that phrase. When the woman to the Priestess' right (normally the Handmaiden) has taken her hand, the Priestess stomps her foot to ground the energy and says, "The Circle is cast. We are now in a Circle between the Worlds. We are here between the realm of the Gods and the land of their people. Here there is all time and no time. We come here to seek the Gods. Blessed be." The Circle responds, "Blessed be," and relax their hands.

Calling in the Quarters/Inviting the Elements

The Elemental spirits are invited to "build the walls of the Circle." Either Priestess walks the Circle deosil (clockwise), beginning in the East, or the person sitting at the Quarter point in each direction may offer the invocation. The group stands as the Priestess (or person calling in the particular direction) lifts her hands and stands in a position symbolizing a pentagram or chalice and says:

"Spirits of the East, Children of Air, who live in the clear home of the hawk and the scythe. Bring us the inspiration of Dawn, the newness of the Spring breeze, the lifting winds that carry us to the skies; grant us the flight of fancy and the joy of soaring. Join us, Spirits of Air."

Everyone bows to the East, and remains facing East as the Priestess offers this meditation on Air:

"On bee spirals
 By the Hawk's eye
Woven in First Breath
And last sigh. Air.
I know."

The same format is followed for each Quarter. The individual invocations and meditations are as follows:

Invocation—
"Spirits of the South, Children of Fire, who thrive in the heated desert, home to lizard and coyote. Bring us the passion of Noonday, the energy of Summer's dance, the quickening fruit of youth that makes sweet our life, the conviction that makes strong our will. Grant us the strength of caring for the quests we choose. Join us, Spirits of Fire."

Meditation—
"By the starfields of firefly sparks,
The candle fire,
Hold fast Love's desire.
I know."

Invocation—
"Spirits of West, Children of Water, who frolic in stream and heaving tides, home of dolphin and trout. Bring us creativity of the sea's boundless diversity, the transforming power of water forced through stone, the deep contemplative satisfaction of Autumn's full harvests. Grant us the power of change as we grow and cycle in our lives. Join us, Spirits of Water."

Meditation—
"Dragonfly dance on bluegreen pond,
Water through rock,
Blood through veins,
All by the Goddess names.
I know."

Invocation—
"Spirits of the North, Children of Earth, who tread the shimmering icy paths of Winter. Bring us the ancient wisdom of secret caves of Earth's beating heart, the renewing power of the cycles ending and beginning all marked by sacred cadence, the wisdom of age and power of knowing. Grant us the wisdom to be well. Join us, Spirits of Earth."

Meditation —
"Cobalt sphere in a black night,
Womb of Earth,
The furies' home,
The webbers' delight.
I know."

The Priestess, either in the East or at her own space in the Circle, says to the Circle, "Repeat after me: I am Air. (response) I am Fire. (response) I am Water. (response) I am Earth. (response) I am all things. (response) All things are me. (response) I am the Goddess' Perfect Child. (response) I am free. (response) Blessed Be."

Invocation of the Goddess and God
Individual invocations should be prepared for the specific Goddess and God pair with which you work (or the Goddess only in Dianic

traditions).

The Priestess raises her hands and offers the invocation to the Goddess, then lights a taper from the Source Candle and with it lights the Goddess candle. The Priestess sitting in the East rings a bell and says, "She is here." The Circle bows to the Goddess.

The Priestess sitting in the East raises her hands and offers the invocation to the God, then lights the God candle. The Priestess in the West rings the bell and says, "He is here." The Circle bows to the God.

The Priestess in the West says, "We are met. Blessed Be." The Circle responds, "Blessed Be," and all sit down.

Stating the Intent

"We have met here to celebrate the New Moon and to make New Moon Vows. Is there other business to come before the Circle?" Should anyone present wish for help in a particular endeavor or spell, or wish to bless jewelry, altar tools, etc., she so states at this time. The Priestess directs the flow of events, and in most cases she has been approached prior to the Circle about any additions to the Work of the Circle. Copper Key operates with a high degree of consensus, but technically the Priestess may decline a request or suggest a more appropriate time for the spell or activity.

Work of the Circle

This includes the New Moon Vows and any other work determined by the Priestess and the Coven during the statement of intent. New Moon Vows are those things which can be reasonably accomplished in a lunar cycle, and are often things which serve to remind us of our commitment to the Gods. These Vows are usually something mundane, such as "Write the first three pages of a brief," or "Hang up a new bird feeder." Sometimes they are more serious — one member of Copper Key vowed to quit smoking and succeeded! Since these vows are made before the Coven, each member is free to encourage her sisters in the keeping of Vows. This custom is the subject of much humor in our group. To deliver her Vow, each member in turn forms a triangle with her hands and focuses on the flame of the Source Candle through it, then says, "For the next lunar cycle, I vow to _____. So mote it be." The Circle responds, "So mote it be."

Note: for a Full Moon, Vows are replaced with Wishes, as the Full Moon is said to be the time for making them. Some members of the Coven choose to make wishes that reinforce their Vows for that lunar cycle, and others ask for things from the improbable (I want Ed McMahon to knock on my door) to the probable (I hope my entry in the art competition wins first place).

Raising a Cone of Power

This is usually done when there are only members of the Coven or Circle present, as the members are tuned up to work with one another. A Cone of Power is raised to add force and energy to the magic and vows which were just completed. This power is raised by chanting, singing, drumming, howling, dancing, or any other appropriate shared experience. The power is raised by all and grounded by the Priestess.

Wine & Cakes
Opening the Circle

The Coven stands. The Priestess raises her hands and says:

> "Sweet Mother, Sister, Daughter,
> Goddess of a Thousand Names,
> Who speaks by shining stars and suckling child,
> Wild winds and sweet dreaming,
> We thank You for Your presence in our Circle tonight and the gifts You daily grant us. We ask that our hearts touch Yours as we extinguish this candle. We bid You Hail and Farewell."

She then damps the wick with a candle snuffer or her Athame, and the Circle responds, "Hail and Farewell," and bows to the Goddess.

The Priestess raises her hands and says:

> "Consort, Brother, Friend, Lover,
> Protector and kin for a thousand years
> Who dances with joy and passion in our lives and in our dreams,
> We thank You for Your presence in our Circle and the gifts you daily grant us. We ask that our hearts touch yours as we extinguish this candle. We bid you Hail and Farewell."

She damps the God Candle, and the Circle responds, "Hail and Farewell," and bows to the God.

The Priestess walks deosil to the East, raises her hands, and says:
> *"Spirits of the East, Children of Air, we thank you for your presence in our Circle and for the gifts of inspiration and new beginnings that you daily bring us. We ask that our spirits touch you as we bid you Hail and Farewell."*

The Circle responds, *"Hail and Farewell,"* and bows to the East.

The Priestess walks deosil to the South, raises her hands, and says:
> *"Spirits of the South, Children of Fire, we thank you for your presence in our Circle and for the gifts of passion and will that you daily bring us. We ask that our spirits touch you as we bid you Hail and Farewell."*

The Circle responds, *"Hail and Farewell,"* and bows to the South.

The Priestess walks deosil to the West, raises her hands, and says:
> *"Spirits of the West, Children of Water, we thank you for your presence in our Circle and for the gifts of change and nurturing that you daily bring us. We ask that our spirits touch you as we bid you Hail and Farewell."*

The Circle responds, *"Hail and Farewell,"* and bows to the West.

The Priestess walks deosil to the North, raises her hands, and says:
> *"Spirits of the North, Children of Earth, we thank you for your presence in our Circle and for the gifts of wisdom and renewal that you daily bring us. We ask that our spirits touch you as we bid you Hail and Farewell."*

The Circle responds, *"Hail and Farewell,"* and bows to the North.

With her Athame pointed toward the ground, the Priestess walks widdershins (counterclockwise) around the Circle and says, "Weave and spin from this place between the worlds to sink safely into the Earth from whence you came. Be renewed and be one with the Mother." When the Priestess returns to the East, she says, "May the peace of the Goddess dwell in your heart. Merry Meet, and Merry Part, and Merry Meet again." Everyone hugs each member of the group.

Post Circle

The rest of the cakes, wine/juice, and whatever other snacks were brought to share are consumed (generally quite wholeheartedly!) and administrative business is discussed, such as the date, time, and location of the next meeting. This business should not be conducted during the actual Circle (most people need to locate calendars, pens, etc.).

ACACIA'S SABBAT SCRIPT

The following ritual script was organized by Acacia for Copper Key's celebration of the Spring Equinox, 1992. The format is general enough to be followed or changed around to suit any celebration. Substituting names of members of your own group for those in the script will help each person keep up with her responsibilities.

As Copper Key was on a road trip to a state park and had the use of several cabins, the bath was set up in one, the feast prepared in another, and the ritual itself took place outdoors next to a bonfire between the two. Space and time limitations may be a consideration when adapting this ritual for your own use.

Acacia and Foxfire served in the traditional Priest & Priestess roles, Acacia sitting in the West facing East, and Foxfire sitting in the East facing West. As Copper Key had decided that the group would be open to women only, a woman would, naturally, fulfill the parts of the ritual usually reserved for the Priest. For this reason, some of the standard Wiccan ritual found in many sources was rewritten by the women to reflect their situation. Instead of an emphasis on masculine/feminine duality, parts of the ritual refer to the Sun and the Moon, Light and Dark, etc.

Ritual Bath (set up by Ginger, River, & Branwen)

Challenge (Laurel)
Using the Staff, as detailed in *Elements of Copper Key Ritual Celebrations.(See page 64.)*

Group Meditation (Acacia)

As the Spring Equinox had been the first Sabbat celebrated by Copper Key, the meditation focused on the cyclical nature of life and the Wheel of the Year. Acacia chose to use a tape of water sounds (rain, waterfall, ocean, etc.) as a background for the meditation, and wrote a simple outline to follow, comparing each person to a drop of water that travels from a rain cloud to the Earth and flows down the streams and river to the ocean, eventually evaporating back to the clouds.

Welcome & Introductions

Acacia and Foxfire introduce themselves to the group by their Craft names; each person around the circle does the same. Guests and members who have not chosen one simply state their mundane name. Acacia welcomes all the guests to Copper Key and explains a little about the ritual. Guests are asked to follow the example of the Coven members when an action or response is called for.

Sweep (Hannah)

She makes the Circle three times, clockwise. The group is instructed by Acacia to visualize all negativity being swept away from the Circle. When Hannah has gone around three times, she leaves the broom in the East and returns to her seat clockwise.

Cleansing & Asperges

Using the Athame, Acacia holds the blade in the dish of Water, and says: "Spirits of the West, Children of Water, cleanse us of all negativity, all insecurity, all fear. So mote it be." Group responds, "So mote it be."

Again using the Athame, Acacia holds the tip of the blade in the dish of Salt, and says: "Spirits of the North, Creatures of the Earth, lend us your strength and stability. So mote it be." Group responds, "So mote it be."

With the Athame, Acacia mixes three bladefuls of Salt into the Water, and says: "Salt joins to Water, as night and day join at the horizon, as we all join to the Universe." With each bladeful, Foxfire rings the bell.

Foxfire takes the taper, lights it from the Union candle, then lights the South candle, saying, "Spirits of the South, Children of Fire, lend us your warmth and inspiration." Acacia rings the bell.

Foxfire then lights the incense with the taper and says, "Spirits of the East, Children of Air, give us the breath of creativity." Acacia rings the bell; Foxfire says, "As Fire and Air have been joined, so too are the Moon and the Sun, so are we all to the Universe."

Beginning in the East, each Element is passed around the Circle:

East: incense—Foxfire says, "Breath the sweet air which fills our lungs and gives us life."

South: candle—Foxfire says, "Feel the warmth which lights our lives and gives us life."

West: water—Acacia says, "Feel the blood of Mother Earth which makes up our bodies and gives us life."

North: salt—Acacia says, "Taste the Earth which purifies all and gives us life."

Casting the Circle
Everyone stands and faces the altar; Acacia takes the Wand and walks clockwise to the East. From that point, she walks around the circle three times deosil (*with the sun,* clockwise).

Calling the Quarters
Again beginning in East and proceeding deosil, Acacia, facing out, says: "Guardians of the East, Spirits of Air, make yourselves known to us here tonight, witness and bless our rites."

Acacia turns and faces the Altar; to call attention to the aspects of that direction, she states, "East, Springtime, East, Yellow, East, Creation, East, Life," and pauses a moment before continuing around the Circle to the South.

Facing out at South, Acacia says, "Guardians of the South, Spirits of Fire, make yourselves known to us here tonight, witness and bless our rites."

Acacia turns and faces the Altar; to call attention to the aspects of that direction, she states, "South, Summer, South, Red, South, Inspiration, South, Life, " and pauses as before.

Facing out at West, Acacia says, "Guardians of the West, Spirits of Water, make yourselves known to us tonight, witness and bless our rites."

Acacia turns and faces the Altar; to call attention to the aspects of that direction, she states, "West, Autumn, West, Blue, West, Depth, West, Life."

Facing out at North, Acacia says, "Guardians of the North, Spirits of Earth, make yourselves known to us here tonight, witness and bless our rites."

Acacia turns and faces the Altar; to call attention to the aspects of that direction, she states, "North, Winter, North, Green, North, Strength, North, Life."

Acacia then says, "The Circle is open." She and Foxfire hug; Acacia returns to the West deosil.

Calling the Gods

Acacia says, "The union of the God and Goddess, the union of Light and Dark, the union of Night and Day are symbolized by the Source Candle on our altar, and we recognize that They are with us always. We symbolize our recognition of Their presence by lighting a candle for the Goddess and the God."

Taking the taper and lighting it from the Union/Source Candle, Acacia says, "Moon Goddess, Mother, sister, help us see your presence in our lives. Please witness and bless these rites." She lights the Goddess candle; Foxfire rings the bell three times. Acacia passes the candle to Foxfire, who passes the bell to Acacia.

Foxfire says, "Sun God, Father, Brother, help us see your presence in our lives. Please witness and bless these rites." She lights the candle, and Acacia rings the bell three times.

Acacia and Foxfire say, "Blessed Be," and the group responds "Blessed Be." Everyone sits down.

Statement of Intent

Acacia says, "We are here tonight to celebrate the Vernal Equinox, Ostara. We also celebrate the friendship of this Circle and the company of our guests."

Business of the Circle

1) *Blessing of the eggs.* At Ostara, it is a tradition to take two eggs, dyed red with food coloring, and throw them into a body of water. This is supposed to insure that the fish will return. In today's environmental crisis, wish for the return of life to polluted waters or the continued preservation of the body of water into which the eggs are tossed following the ritual.

2) *Blessing of the seeds.* A packet of herb seeds is passed, and each person takes a seed for each vow or goal they wish to attain in this Season (up until Beltane, the next Sabbat). Pots or recycled plastic containers full of soil are passed to each person from the North. Going in a circle from the East, each person speaks aloud their goal/vow and plants the seeds in their containers.

3) If any member has a particular need or wishes to add an additional work to the business of the Circle, it should be done here. (A coven which has been working together for a long period of time may wish to raise some energy with chanting, singing, or dancing, and ground the energy for some mutually agreed-upon goal. This would not be appropriate if there are guests present.)

Circle Sharing

Mythological stories about Ostara are shared; herbalism is discussed; members share any concerns, problems, or triumphs they may have had since the last meeting.

Wine and Cakes

Acacia takes the Athame and the Chalice to the East. She and Foxfire symbolically represent the physical union of the Goddess and God with the Chalice and the Athame, as follows:

Foxfire kneels, holding the Chalice up. Acacia holds the Athame over the open Chalice and then puts the tip into the wine. The two say the following:

Acacia: As the Moon rules the night,

Foxfire: So the Sun rules the day,

Both:	And without them both we would be left in darkness.
Acacia:	In their union do we find the cycle of life, death, & rebirth,
Foxfire:	And so in our lives are the Gods revealed.
Both:	From the Goddess and the God do we all proceed, their children and humble servants. Blessed Be.
All:	Blessed Be.

Foxfire stands. Acacia picks up the plate of Cakes. With the Athame, she takes some of the wine and sprinkles it over the Cakes, saying, "May the Gods bless the farmers who grew the wheat, the millers who made the flour, the bakers who baked these cakes, and all who partake of them tonight."

A cake is put into the Libation Bowl and some of the wine is poured over it.

Taking a piece of cake, Acacia feeds it to Foxfire, saying, "May you never know hunger." She then takes the Chalice and puts it Foxfire's lips to drink, saying, "May you never know thirst." Foxfire repeats this for Acacia. Then they proceed to each member of the Circle to share Wine and Cakes.

Closing
Acacia returns to the West, and facing the altar, says:
> "Our Lady and Lord, Spirits of the Four Directions, we ask that you stay with us as we celebrate this night and this fellowship, and that at the first light of dawn you return to the World of the Gods, your beautiful realms. We vow to stay ever mindful of your place in our daily lives, and we thank you for the gifts of love, of strength, of light, of warmth, of creativity, of inspiration, of friendship, and the gift of life. Blessed Be." Everyone exchanges hugs with each person around the Circle.

Feast
The first portion of each dish is put into the libation bowl (or another bowl, if the altar bowl is too small to accommodate this). Following

the meal, the libation bowl(s) is taken away from the area in which the group is meeting and the contents are left under a tree or in a clearing. This is an offering to the Gods and all the Spirits of Nature, a thank-you for the blessings that they bestow upon each of us.

Vigil

JOURNAL ENTRIES

1. Orchid's essay brought up these issues for me:

2. After imagining myself at Ginger's meeting, I think I would have felt this way if I had been there:

3. Would I be more comfortable with Co-Priestesses, as Acacia and Foxfire at Spring Equinox, or with a Priestess and Priest? How do I feel about the duality of energy being present in a Circle? How do I feel about myself—do I have both male and female energy within me?

4. How easy would it be for me to get involved in someone else's ritual? Would I mind participating as requested in the chanting, the ritual gestures, the vows, etc.?

5. Would I feel more comfortable meeting with a group that has been established for a long period of time, or would I prefer to meet with a group whose membership might change from meeting to meeting? How would I feel if members of my own Circle wanted to bring guests to certain rituals or activities?

6. When the ritual script calls for inviting in the Goddess and God, for calling in the Quarters, I think that really means this:

7. Here, in my own words, is how I would ask in the Goddess and God:

COPPER KEY RECOMMENDS:

Ariadne's Thread: A Workbook of Goddess Magic, by Shekhinah Mountainwater; Freedom, California: The Crossing Press, ©1988.

Casting the Circle: A Woman's Book of Ritual, by Diane Stein; Freedom, California: The Crossing Press, ©1990.

A Witches Bible Compleat, by Janet & Stewart Farrar; New York: Magickal Childe, ©1991.

Cakes for the Queen of Heaven, by Shirley A. Ranck; Boston: Unitarian Universalist Association, ©1986.

5
LIVING
THE WHEEL

MER-NUIT'S STORY

I GREW up in a house full of negative energy. I am not talking about a dysfunctional family (we functioned okay), I'm talking about the presence of spirits. On the surface we were a white-collar, suburban Catholic family, but there was a wild Celtic streak from my mother's mother that undermined all that. I grew up hearing stories about spirits that communicated by knocking on Grandma's headboard, a Banshee—like Great Grandma who returned in dreams to warn us of approaching death in the family, of communications received through Ouija boards and spirit writing. My own bedroom was so haunted no one would walk down the hallway at night. Even in broad daylight, sometimes the bad vibes drove family members to sit out on the front porch rather than sit inside, *alone*. We used to beg our parents to have a priest exorcise the house, but they never did. I think they were too embarrassed.

By the time I was a teenager, I was already reading about the occult, studying Tarot and experimenting with meditation and astral projection. A classic case of what Dion Fortune would call "psychic attack" soon followed. I suffered from repeated bouts of night terrors, which are basically leaping out of bed and screaming your head off because you think an evil presence is in the room trying to kill you.

After I left home, I very rarely had such attacks, until several years ago when I started to study Wicca. Immediately, I noticed a pattern—mystical Full Moon rituals would be followed by nightmares; a heavy-duty Tarot reading would be begging for a full-blown screaming dream. With great dismay, I began to suspect that I was an unstable personality who shouldn't dabble in the spirit world. I feared having a nervous breakdown.

❖❖❖

From my dream journal, December 1991:

I am being threatened by an evil presence. I grab an iron Athame with both hands and slash a large pentagram in the direction of danger. Beautiful sparks of white light shoot from the tip of the blade. I wake and feel more positive about the Craft then I have in months. Interpretation: I have the tools I need to protect myself. I take this dream as a signal to learn more about the Craft. It is a positive path that can help me deal with the psychic world.

My friend Ginger had an iron Athame like the one in my dream. I told her, "Now I just need to get an Athame like yours and I'll be okay."

We celebrated Copper Key's first Yule at Laurel's big Victorian house. There were about 25 people there, including friends and family of the Coven. I brought my daughter, Tasha, to her first Circle. Laurel's three-year-old swept the Circle, dressed in a little green shift. Laurel and her husband Seal served as Priestess and Priest, leading us through a solemn Gardnerian-style rite that had now become familiar, though it had once seemed so bizarre. Laurel asked me to call in the North. I was in a state of panic, because I suffer from stage fright. I had been practicing my little invocation like mad, calling to the North to shelter our dreams as she shelters the sleeping seed. When my part was over, I could relax and enjoy the ritual.

It was a night of song and laughter, of candles and sparklers and good food and fun and presents. We had decided to exchange home-made gifts, and I had produced a little booklet on Yule traditions that had been a real labor of love. That Yule beat all the Christian Christmases I had had as a child, though the gifts were simple—a jar of homemade bath salts from Moriah, a crystal Diana had dug on a trip to Arkansas, a sage smudge stick Acacia had grown and bound, a shell necklace made by Branwen and Hannah from shells they found on one of Copper Key's weekend trips together.

Then Ginger and Laurel showed me their joint gift to me—an iron Athame. I was overwhelmed. I had determined to scrimp and save to buy one, no matter what. I couldn't believe their generosity. The Athame would go under my pillow that night, an old Celtic tradition to keep away nightmares. And I felt that it was also a symbol of dedication to study, to stay the course, to continue the spiritual journey, and to do it without fear.

One thing I remember about that night, sitting and looking around the Circle at the faces of my friends, including two guests I had brought to see what our Coven was all about, was how proud I was of us. This was a good religious tradition, a beautiful practice, so healthy and healing. It made me sad to think that we had to be so secretive about it, so worried of what the neighbors would think if they knew a Witches' Coven was holding a Sabbat next door. It made me resolve to fight back against this religious persecution by helping found a CUUPs[1] chapter at the local Unitarian Church so that we Pagans would have a place to worship in freedom (but that is another story).

It has been over a year since that wonderful Yule. Copper Key has been through a lot of changes since then. I have continued to study and use techniques in Wicca and other magical traditions to keep all evil out and let good enter in. When bad vibes collect, I do a simple house blessing with sage and water and sweeping. That and a classic white light meditation seem to keep everything under control. I can't remember the last time I had night terrors, but if and when I do, I have the tools I need to protect myself.

---

[1] CUUPs - Covenant of Unitarian Universalist Pagans (see Appendix 2).

MEMORABLE MEETINGS

IN RELATING the celebrations and meetings of Copper Key over the months before they took Covenstead, it is important to remember that they often combined New or Full Moon meetings with special occasions in the lives of the members of the Circle, as well as occasionally combining a Lunar meeting with a Sabbat. (Typically in Wiccan traditions, a celebration may occur three days before or after the actual Lunar event or holiday.)

Sabbats are perfect occasions around which to build retreats and extended meetings. For instance, at Mabon, which is considered in many traditions the Witch's Thanksgiving, Copper Key set out for a lakeside cabin with a big kitchen, and every member brought food to share. Being out of the city and planning in advance to spend the night at the cabin opened up a whole evening for the celebration of the ritual: no one was worried about driving home late at night or getting up the next morning for work. They were therefore more relaxed and able to focus on the event. If your group is unable to get out of town, plan a whole Saturday or Sunday to spend together celebrating holidays.

The following section will take you through the first year-and-a-day and up to Covenstead with Copper Key, discussing the meetings as they happened. You may glean ideas for your own celebrations from their experience. While this calendar does not include the text of every ritual performed by Copper Key, a basic Moon Ritual and a Sabbat Script are provided in Chapter IV; below are elements added to the basic format which individualized each meeting.

The very first meeting of what would become Copper Key was the Full Moon of February, 1991. "But we sort of date the formation

of the group from Ostara," Laurel said. This calendar will begin with
Ostara, the Vernal Equinox, of 1991.

MARCH

Well before the group came to think of themselves as a Coven, they
were a Circle. And before they decided to close the Circle to women
only, they attempted to include husbands, boyfriends, acquain-
tances, and other men in the celebrations. This integration had a very
limited success. Many of the members felt the energy of the Circle
was radically different when men were present. Perhaps the men felt
this too; in fact, no men showed up for the ritual portion of the Ostara
celebration, but some did join in for the celebration following the
ritual.

Ostara is the time of the year in the Northern hemisphere when
new life is emerging, seeds are planted, and people and animals are
coming out of their Winter inwardness. For the ritual celebration, the
women met at the bookstore and set up the altar with many of the
Pagan elements that have been adopted by the Western world as
Easter decorations: rabbits, nests, and eggs, in pinks, yellows, and
greens.

Acacia served as Priestess and led the group through a ritual
drawn from the Hidden Grove Tradition. In addition, she brought a
bowl of potting soil, an empty paper egg carton, forget-me-not flower
seeds, and two eggs dyed red with natural food coloring.

During the Work of the Circle, the bowl of dirt and the seeds
were consecrated (passed around the Circle and blessed by the
Elements: i.e., passed through the smoke of the incense in the East,
passed over the candle flame in the South, sprinkled with water in the
West, rubbed with a stone in the North, and presented to the Goddess
and God in the center of the altar). Then each member took a spoonful
of dirt, filled a space in the egg carton with it, picked out as many seeds
as they had wishes for the upcoming season of growth, and planted
them. Foxfire was given the entire carton to take to her farm to plant
in the area where she hoped the group would later set up a permanent
ritual space.

The red eggs, one for the Goddess and one for the God, were blessed and held in reserve for the next part of the evening. A few members called their various spouses and friends to join them at a riverbank near their city. By the time the destination was reached, there were four couples and four cars. The area the group chose was a notorious lover's lane.

"When we got down to the river there were five or six couples already parked there. We arrived in four different cars," Laurel said. "We pull in, park our cars together, and get out. By then the couples are getting a little interested in us. Then we walk to the edge of the river, stand in a circle, chant, and start chucking stuff over the banks into the river. By then the couples who were watching all started their engines and left as quickly as possible."

They threw the two red eggs into the river, which was already beginning to swell with the Spring thaw. This stems from a Pagan tradition of waking up the fish so that there will be plenty for the upcoming year. In this day of environmental devastation, the Circle asked that the eggs bring healing to the polluted waters.

APRIL

The Full Moon of April and the Sabbat known as Beltane (May 1st) were within three days of one another in 1991. Copper Key planned a huge outdoor celebration at Foxfire's farm. Beltane recounts the courtship and first coupling of the Goddess and God; it is a true fertility festival. The May Day celebrations in Western Europe (even to some degree in the Catholic Church) harken back to the days when youth was venerated on this day. A May Queen and King were chosen, and the people made love in the fields to insure the success of the year's crops.

However, Copper Key was unable to get to Foxfire's because of a rainstorm that lasted most of the week prior to the celebration. Instead they met at the bookstore, where River served as Priestess. As it was indoors, there was not room for the traditional Maypole celebration or a bonfire over which to jump, but the group made do. River shared stories from the British Isles and cut an apple in half widthwise, revealing the pentacle inside. The apple was passed around the Circle for everyone to take a bite from, and those members who were hoping to conceive during that year bit into the core of the apple and swallowed a seed whole.

MAY

Tara served as Priestess for the Full Moon of May, 1991, again celebrated at the bookstore. As it was mutually agreed that when serving as Priestess a member could determine the type of ritual to be celebrated, Tara led the group through its first truly Dianic Circle, where only the Goddess was invited in and the group focused solely on feminine energy.

Using the colors of the rainbow as her guide, Tara associated each color with particular attributes and aspects of various Goddesses from around the world. For example, the color purple represents change and is to be associated with Goddesses of change and rebirth. Tara used her individual strengths, such as her gentle voice and her gift for storytelling, to move the Circle through grounding, relaxation, meditation, and awareness. She closed the Work of the Circle with a naming and self-blessing ritual, for which she had set out small dishes of water and scented oil for each member. She also presented each woman with a woven friendship bracelet onto which were sewn five tiny cloth Goddess figures.

JUNE

As of June, 1991, the Circle decided to meet on both Full and New Moons, as well as the eight Sabbats. Attendance had grown by leaps and bounds, as word of mouth and referrals from the bookstore brought more and more women to the Circles. So as not to wear out their welcome, Copper Key decided to meet once monthly at the bookstore and to hold other meetings in their homes.

New Moons were designated for ritual and teachings on various subjects, which members agreed to research and provide. Acacia and Laurel served as Priestesses for the New Moon, which was held at Tara's. Six to eight people were expected to attend, as the meeting was in a private home and no one thought that first-time visitors would want to make the trip. Instead, upwards of fourteen people crowded into Tara's living room, many of whom neither Laurel nor Acacia had ever met. But to their surprise, they had enough of everything for those present. Instead of the traditional blessing of the elements, flowers were passed around and their scent represented Air; grapes were eaten so that each woman could experience Water; warm, malleable wax was passed around to represent Fire; and pieces of downfall soda-straw rock from inside a cave were distributed to each woman to represent Earth.

The teaching of the evening was in two parts, the first being the Wheel of the Year, which Laurel and Acacia led, and the second, after the Circle was complete and the feast eaten, was led by Moriah. She taught the group the Miserloo, a Greek dance in honor of the Snake Goddess.

Litha, combined with the Full Moon, was celebrated on Foxfire's farm, and even more women attended. Twenty women hiked out into the woods where Foxfire had cleared an area inside a grove of trees. Each woman was asked to bring a rock to leave in the Circle to designate the boundary of the area as a sacred space. Dogs, cats, horses, even a raccoon or two passed near where the women met. Ahriel, a young woman of seventeen who had met the group through River, served as Priestess with River's assistance. This was particularly appropriate for the holiday, as young female energy is the mythological focal point of Midsummer. As the Sun went down and the Moon rose, the women sang and chanted to honor the full moon. River led the "Aradia" chant:

> "Full Moon, shining bright,
> Midnight on the water,
> O, Aradia,
> Diana's Silver Daughter."

Following the ritual, the women hiked back to Foxfire's house and feasted on dishes made with honey, eggs, and cheese, and some drank a honey liqueur which substituted for mead, the traditional drink of Litha.

JULY

The first big administrative vote of Copper Key was held at the Full Moon of July, 1991. At this meeting, the group recognized the need to have time for members to bond, time to meet new potential members, and times for special things reserved only for the Circle. Copper Key opened Full Moon meetings to members only ("grandmothering" anyone who had already been coming to meetings) and decided to hold them in individual homes. They opened New Moon meetings to visitors and decided to continue holding them in the bookstore, and also decided that they would each sew or have made a special robe to wear to closed meetings. As the group decided that they were not ready to meet Skyclad, the robe served to take the women out of their mundane clothes and give their meetings a sense of otherworldliness. It was also decided that regular meetings would be open to women only, and that the group would designate those special occasions to which men could be invited.

It was also during July that the first emergency meeting was called, and the first healing work was done in the Circle. Sjöö, a friend of Briar's who had been meeting with the group off and on for a few months, was the victim of acquaintance rape. Sjöö turned to Copper Key for help, and asked for a healing ritual.

Tara agreed to serve as Priestess. Her affinity for the Dianic tradition made the planning of the ritual itself essentially an easier task, as the healing of all aspects of the Goddesses of the world were called upon. However, even though Tara preferred to lead Dianic rituals, she determined that Sjöö would need the comfort of a safe, positive masculine spirit, and so she called in the God in His aspects of father and protector. Sjöö and Briar also had a male Wiccan friend who was invited to attend the Circle. He was gifted in music and brought with him a Celtic harp. His playing provided a beautiful, soft background to the ritual.

The women of Copper Key brought with them small talismans for Sjöö to keep which were charged with qualities such as protection and peace and consecrated during the Circle. The ritual asked that the energy inflicted upon Sjöö be mirrored back to its source, the rapist, as the negativity originated there and there should return. This walks the fine line of harming none, but the group decided that the violence of the crime was not their creation, and that no one in the group, Sjöö included, should have to own that which was forced upon her.

One of the gifts presented to Sjöö was a necklace on which were strung several different figurines of women, each with body language and facial expression personifying a different emotion, from joy to rage and everything in between. Copper Key told Sjöö that her own emotions were her key to healing, and that the women of the Circle would be there for her as she experienced each one.

AUGUST

Sjöö's healing Circle gave way to healing work in other meetings. In August of 1991, Diana and Tara were planning the teaching for the New Moon, as they had both studied astrology and were working up the charts of each member of the Circle. In spending time together working on this project, they discovered that they also had something in common—they were both trying to disentangle themselves from bad love relationships. Following their New Moon teaching, they asked the Circle to do an unbinding for them both, where they would through ritual leave the bad relationships behind and would be able to move on with their emotional lives.

Laurel and Moriah planned the unbinding ritual and served as Priestesses. At the start of the work of the Circle, Diana and Tara wrote on pieces of paper those aspects of the relationships (such as co-dependency, unfaithfulness, etc.) that they wanted out of their lives permanently. Then the Priestesses literally bound the wrists of Diana and Tara with silk cord. The two women read the things they wanted out of their lives out loud to the Circle, and dropped them into a cauldron with a burning coal in it. Once the papers had burned, the women of the Circle each told both Tara and Diana the individual traits about them that they admired, respected, and loved; positive things which could serve as a foundation on which to rebuild their self-esteem. At that point, Laurel and Moriah cut the cords and dropped them into the cauldron to burn as well.

Also at that meeting, Laurel and Moriah did a house blessing for Branwen's new apartment. First, leaving Branwen in the front room, the group went through the house with drums, rattles, bells, and candles to drive out any negative energy that might have been left by the previous occupants. Then the group went through with oil to bless the doors and windows, a smudge stick to fill the air with sacred smoke, and an herbal infusion to bless the space. Laurel sprinkled the rooms of the apartment with an infusion made from the following herbs, using a sprig of Rue as an aspergillum:

> Parsley for purification;
> Sage for protection;
> Roses for luck;
> Mint for riches;
> Lemon balm for health;
> Rosemary for magic;
> Lavender for happiness;
> Basil for love; and
> Pennyroyal for peace.

SEPTEMBER

The New Moon of September was Ginger's first Circle as Priestess. She had been participating along with several other women in the Circle in a Cakes for the Queen of Heaven class at the Unitarian Universalist Church and used a good deal of material from that curriculum to plan the ritual. At one point Ginger led the group in an exercise taken from the Cakes curriculum where everyone sings to each individual member while that person must sit, be still, and listen:

> "(Name of member), you are beautiful.
> (Name of member), you are strong.
> Wonderful to be with, carry us along.
> (Name of member), hear our loving song."

Also at that meeting (open to guests, as it was a New Moon), the group adopted the wearing of name tags upon which were written their Circle names, and no mundane names were used before, during, or after the ritual. This also helped the members to remember their Sisters' chosen names.

Mabon (the Fall Equinox) and the Full Moon of September fell on the same date in 1991. The women of Copper Key planned their first retreat for that weekend, and a house on a lake was made available for their use. The women decided to invite significant others and friends for the weekend. This was the first exposure many husbands and friends had to the Circle and to Wicca. After arriving and unpacking on Friday night, the Circle left the menfolk and other friends in the cabin and walked by candlelight down to the water's edge.

A packing box was set up with a soft blanket inside. One by one, each member of Copper Key was closed up inside the box and a heartbeat rhythm was played for several seconds on a drum. "It was at first sort of scary, although I think it was probably meant to be. The changes I was making in my life were profound and they are scary. This ritual was really an act of trust in the women I called my sisters," Ginger said.

After the heartbeat rhythm had been played for several seconds, the box was opened and the member pulled out by her Circlemates — each of them was a "Born Again Pagan." Each was given a password to use exclusively with Copper Key and a tiny pendant that symbolized the Circle; then she was led out into the Full Moonlight to spend some time thinking about her own path. Each member then threw a rock into the water representing things about her old life that she wished to leave behind, and threw a flower into the water stating her chosen Craft name.

Waiting for them back at the cabin was a huge meal. An added bonus was that their spouses and friends had gotten to know one another in the process of preparing that dinner. Laurel even surprised the group with a fully decorated birthday cake.

The following Saturday afternoon, everyone went to a public beach and collected garbage bags full of trash left behind by the hundreds of people who used the lake during the summer. This was as much a shared ritual as the Mabon Circle later that evening.

"I count that weekend as a true turning point in my life," said Foxfire. "I really felt the community that we were building was a family, and everything about that time seems magical to me." She even volunteered to Priestess her first Circle the following Moon.

OCTOBER

"The Goddess has created us in a beautiful, infinite variety. Let us rejoice in our differences." This is how Foxfire opened the New Moon ceremony October 7th of 1991. She led the group through a meditation focusing on the Earth and the Children of the Earth, and also led prayers for racial and gender harmony, as the news that week was full of violence perpetrated against women and between various ethnic groups. The teaching that night was on "right-brain" activities, and the group tried drawing using their non-dominant hand.

River served as Priestess for the Samhain celebration, which in Wicca is the New Year. She set the altar with fall colors and a large iron cauldron in the middle. She told the story of Persephone's journey into the Underworld and shared a pomegranate around the Circle. This was the first meeting where the members of the Circle wore their new robes.

"Samhain is a very disturbing Sabbat, and it should be," Laurel said. "Very introspective, a lot of serious soul-searching, evaluation. The emphasis on Death does not necessarily mean to rattle up the bones of our ancestors; I think they should be left in peace in whatever cycle they may be. The emphasis on Death is, I think, to remind us that before we know it, this cycle will be over. We came here with something to accomplish, and we'd better reassess and be sure we're on the right path or we're going to be here doing it all over again. I can't think of anything more depressing than standing still or even regressing in our karmic development, and karma is not even a Wiccan word, but it does convey the idea."

While Samhain is traditionally the time for taking stock and getting ready for the introspective winter months, it is also the time to honor those who have died over the previous year, and say goodbye to them until you meet again. One member of the group had lost a daughter to cancer several years earlier, and celebrated her short life by describing her to the members of the Circle. While it would be impossible for her to let go of her daughter altogether, this aspect of the ritual allowed her to share her grief and her love with the other women in the group who were missing someone close to them. It was the first time she had ever told the group about her lost daughter.

Penetrare
(or why Samhain precedes Yule)
by Ginger

The veil is rent!
The Cauldron tilts with
            measured weight of
Ghost grey Spirits;
Abduction
To the Vortex.

Drowned in dizzying flow
Whirlwind dirge, free fall
To the Center.

Returning life,
Breech born anew
Teetering on the Cauldron's lip,
Blood hot,
Dripping sap
Through birth canal and
            creviced scar.

Shadow
On bright snow, the
Solstice cradle.

NOVEMBER

As Wicca is a religion based upon free will, healing cannot occur
unless the person to be healed has asked for it and is aware that the
individual Wiccan or the Circle/Coven is working for that goal. This
is at times difficult to accept. One very powerful work occurred when
Acacia's niece was sexually assaulted by a neighbor. The niece lived
in a different city—her mother was not only a fundamentalist Christian but was also unaware that Acacia had chosen a Wiccan path. "I
felt helpless in the situation. There I was working magic with a Circle

to help so many people, and I couldn't even do anything to help my own niece," she said. "I spent nights crying on people's shoulders until we finally decided that a general spell of protection wouldn't violate her free will or that of her mother."

Acacia and her Circlemates planned to ask the Gods to protect the family from further harm, and particularly to protect her niece as the inevitable exams, treatments, and investigations ensued. The work was done at the November Full Moon Circle, and was the last of three that night. An incense Acacia prepared specially for that part of the ritual was lit. A bowl of saffron water was passed around the Circle so that members could wash their hands before beginning. Acacia brought a simple cloth doll which was passed around, and as each woman held the doll, she spoke aloud her hopes for the child and her prayer that the Gods protect her.

"When that doll went around the Circle, it felt like that doll was alive. It was the first Circle I had ever been in where several people cried, just out of the emotion of the moment, and I felt that a lot of real power was raised," Laurel said. "It was not drumming and chanting and saying, 'Okay, let's raise some power now,' but rather, the group said, 'We are going to will this with our minds, and it is going to happen. We are going to put this healing energy in this inanimate object,' and it was very serious power raising. Everyone was hot and exhausted at the end of the ritual. It was one of the most memorable Circles of that year."

After the doll was passed back to the point of origin, it was consecrated just as a tool or piece of ritual jewelry would be. "Even though they may not have realized the full impact of the care package they received, my niece and her mother appreciated the gift we sent," Acacia added, "and my niece still sleeps with that doll."

DECEMBER

The New Moon for December was "snowed out" in 1991, and by Yule (the Winter Solstice), the flu was ravaging the entire city, including many members of Copper Key. A retreat had to be canceled, and by the time everyone could get together to celebrate in health, it was Saturday the 28th.

Traditions which celebrate the rebirth of the Sun on Winter Solstice are the foundations for the Christmas celebrations in the Western world. The tree, the Yule log, the exchanging of gifts, the myth of the Young God's birth, all predate Christianity. In fact, the early church chose December to celebrate Christ's birth because the Pagans they hoped to make into converts were already celebrating the birth of God at that time.

From Mer-Nuit's essay: "It was a night of song and laughter, of candles and sparklers and good food and fun and presents. We had decided to exchange home-made gifts, and I had produced a little booklet on Yule traditions that had been a real labor of love. That Yule beat all the Christian Christmases I had had as a child, though the gifts were simple—a jar of homemade bath salts from Moriah, a crystal Diana had dug on a trip to Arkansas, a sage smudge stick Acacia had grown and bound, a necklace made by Branwen and Hannah from shells they found on one of Copper Key's weekend trips together." Providing a Pagan-safe place and time to celebrate Yuletide helped the women and their families and friends experience the community they were creating outside the commercial traditions of the society in which they lived.

JANUARY, 1992

While not part of a formal ritual, Ginger hosted a candle-making party for Copper Key at her house. All manner of candles for rituals, altars, shrines, and gifts were made, including charm candles and prosperity candles full of pennies. Books on candle-making were checked out of the local library and everyone chipped in money for the supplies. Unstructured activities such as this allowed Copper Key members to spend time with each other and get to know one another outside formal meetings; over time, such extra curricular events helped cement the bonds between the women. As the second year rolled around, members' personal lives were much more intertwined and the Circle began to spend more and more time together, almost on a daily basis. (Note: clean-up is easier if candles are made outside.)

FEBRUARY

Mer-Nuit, Diana, and Ivy served as Priestesses for Imbolc (Candlemas), 1992. Ginger made garlands of baby's breath for everyone to wear, and the Priestesses made posters of the chants that were to be used that night and hung them on the walls. This is the time of year when baby animals are being born in hibernating dens; "Imbolc" translates as "in the belly," or "quickening." (In some traditions, the Goddess at this time returns from the underworld pregnant with the young Sun God whom she births on Ostara; each group must decide whether to follow the hunting or agricultural Wheel of the Year, or a calendar of holidays completely different from those discussed here.)

Also, divination and internal activities, such as meditation and astral projection, are the magical focus of this time. Diana passed around a bag of Nordic runes, let each member draw one, and helped interpret the meaning for each person during the work of the Circle. Another appropriate activity would be to scry using a liqueur lighted in a cauldron or by using a special mirror.

Scrying Chant
by Ginger

I am
All things.
All things
Are me.

Look
in the mirror,
Say
what you see.

MARCH

As Ostara rolled around again, Copper Key made plans to travel out of town once more as a group. While a complete script of the ritual which Acacia and Foxfire presented to the group can be found in the last chapter, it is important to note that on this trip several guests were present: Laurel's friend who was on the verge of matriculating from Divinity School, an herbalist from another state, a couple (friends of Ginger) who were exploring alternative spirituality, one of Acacia's Pagan friends from another city, and spouses and significant others as well.

Many members of Copper Key recognized at this point that performing ritual for an audience comprised mainly of visitors was not conducive to strengthening the bonds inside the Circle. Rather than being able to focus on their development as a working Circle, the group was instead focused on making the guests comfortable with the ritual and including them in activities for which the visitors had little or no preparation. The strain of continually trying to explain what the group was doing or to discuss, both during ritual and beyond, made the experience a drain on energy.

APRIL

It was in April of '92 that Laurel decided the time had come for her to take a sabbatical from Copper Key. The circumstances surrounding her decision involved her ex-husband and children (although what she most feared—a custody battle—did not come to pass). As a parent, and as a responsible member of the Circle, she did what was best for all concerned. Although she needed the support of her Circle to get through the difficult period she faced, the only way to insure the safety of her children and the safety of the Circle was to stop meeting with Copper Key for a short period. It wasn't an issue whether or not she wished to be a test case for religious freedom. She did not wish her own spiritual path to cause her family and friends any pain and suffering.

MAY

While April may have been fraught with difficulty, May brought positive events in the lives of Copper Key members. When Ivy came to her first meeting the preceding year, she had just learned she was pregnant. This May when she was close to her due date, a ritual was performed in her backyard which focused on a safe delivery and celebrated the coming event. In the middle of the Circle, a pallet of pillows and blankets were laid for Ivy to relax upon. The members of the Circle shared their hopes for her and listened to her concerns. The Circle used "Ring Around the Rosy" as a way to raise energy and ground it all around her; as silly as it may sound, it was an extremely appropriate way to raise a cone of power to seal all the good wishes and hopes for her safety and that of the coming child. Ivy remembers the face of each woman as she danced past; she told Ginger later that the faces seemed to appear and disappear in mid-air, thanks to the candlelight, and that she felt connected with each woman. "In planning the ritual, I was concerned that we not induce early labor," Ginger said. "She wanted a smooth delivery, everything to simply go right. So we imagined an orderly, safe birth for her and for Baby Acorn. Believe what you must, but she had a four-hour labor, and I think it's interesting to note that the doctor wasn't even in the room when the baby came and still all was well."

JUNE

Of all the Circles shared in Copper Key's first two years, perhaps one of the most important was when a member came to the decision to leave the group. Moriah, who had been studying Native American traditions for many years before coming to meet with Copper Key, had at first thought that Wicca was the path calling to her. She thought that she was, indeed, a Witch. She had formed close friendships with the women of Copper Key; she and her husband had both been on road trips and had come to the open Circles. But something was nagging at her; she realized she was staying with the group more for the friendships than for the religion. After many months of agonizing about it, she finally called a Circle at her home in which to discuss her feelings. It was at this meeting that the other members of the group finally said out loud that yes, they were going to be a Wiccan group exclusively, that they wanted to take Covenstead, and that, although they still wanted to include other traditions in their broad network of friends and contacts, only rituals which fell within the realms of European Wicca would be practiced. On hearing their decision, Moriah decided to discontinue her membership in Copper Key, but not to lose the companions that she had found there. The importance of opening discussion about her misgivings and having a formal chance to say goodbye to the Circle cannot be stressed enough; closure in the formal relationship helped Moriah and members of Copper Key to remain friends.

For Litha, the Sabbat which celebrates Midsummer, Mer-Nuit wrote the following guided meditation:

> "It is Midsummer. You are walking in the woods. You are the Witch of these woods. You know the trees, in all their leafy green beside the narrow path. The birds in the trees seem to know you as they dart here and there. You walk alone. You are striding forward with a sure step.
>
> You are moving towards your goal; you feel good, in balance, in harmony with the world. The wheel of fortune is turning, the forces are in motion, forces you have helped to set in spin by your actions, your will, your words.
>
> You are carrying something in a little pine box. You are carrying something from your past that you need to get rid of. Something old and unwanted, maybe something that gave you pain, that gave you stress. You will be happier without this baggage. You have wanted to get rid of this for some time.
>
> You come to a crossroads, a powerful place. Here in the Earth you set down the box, and you begin to dig. You feel the Earth, smell the good smell, see the color, feel the texture . . . . when the hole is big enough, you place the box in it.
>
> Bury the box, cover it with Earth, pack it tight. The Earth has the power and strength to hold this miserable thing. You will not see it again.
>
> You turn and leave, feeling lighter, feeling positive, feeling a fortunate child of the Goddess.
>
> You see a light ahead of you, through the dark trees. It is the candle in our Circle. You come forward and take your place in the Circle, and open your eyes."

JULY

Nearly three months after Copper Key had been meeting for a year-and-a-day, the Circle finally took Covenstead. Laurel returned to Copper Key at this time, and she, Acacia, and Ginger planned a simple celebration to mark the Covenstead. In it, the tokens given to each woman at Mabon were replaced with a more substantial talisman, and the women took new Craft names for themselves to mark their progress in the Coven; the group even discussed changing the name of the Circle to denote the changes they were accepting, although it was decided that they would remain Copper Key.

Also at that meeting two new members were asked to pledge a year-and-a-day to learning if they were to be a part of the Coven. Both women (Orchid and Sabina) accepted the offer.

In learning to be a Coven, the women of Copper Key Circle had to accept change as a fundamental part of life and to accept the humanity of one another as well as the divinity. They continue to celebrate holidays and lunar events as well as milestones in one another's lives and to share their spiritual beliefs within the context of the religious community they created.

JOURNAL ENTRIES

1. I wish I had been there at this meeting of Copper Key, because:

2. These are the most important three celebrations of which I have been a part to this date and why:

3. Which one celebration of an entire year do I feel most drawn to Priestess? Why?

4. This is how reading Mer-Nuit's story made me feel:

5. Starting today, I will keep a record of all my own Circle's meetings here in my journal.

COPPER KEY RECOMMENDS:

Books:

Ancient Ways: Reclaiming Pagan Traditions, by Pauline Campanelli; St. Paul: Llewellyn Publications, ©.

Celebrating Life: Rites of Passage for All Ages, by Tzipora Klein; Oak Park, Illinois: Delphi Press, © 1992.

Wheel of the Year: Living the Magical Life, by Pauline Campanelli; St. Paul: Llewellyn Publications, ©.

Tapes:

CHANTS: Ritual Music of the Reclaiming Community, chants written (and sung) by such notable women as Starhawk, Z. Budapest, and Shekinah Mountainwater. To order, write Reclaiming Chants, P.O. Box 14404, San Francisco, California, 94114.

Lunar Calendars:
Try your local bookstore, or write to the following:

Johnson Books	Snake & Snake Productions
1880 South 57th Court	Route 3, Box 165
Boulder, Colorado 80301	Durham, North Carolina 27713

HAVE COVEN, WILL TRAVEL

HANNAH'S STORY

FINDING PAGANISM has been a very long process. I believe that it has actually been my whole life. Even though my parents don't call themselves Pagans, they have always taught us that there is something very strong in the force of Nature. When I was a little kid they allowed me to go to different churches with several friends. Each time I went I felt that I was watching a show. I remember thinking, "Why in the world do they listen to THAT guy up there?" I just never felt right about what I was being told. Answers to questions that they couldn't answer for me, I was finding inside myself, not in the Bible or in church.

Much later, I met Branwen, and we got to talking. The next thing I knew, I was driving through the woods with her and River (whom I had just met an hour before—we were giving her a ride) to a cabin on a lake to celebrate Mabon. I was a little nervous because I had never been around a group of people who shared my views, much less attended a ritual. But I was never scared of what I might find. And the minute we arrived and I met all of Copper Key, something happened. I was completely comfortable. Generally, I am very nervous and shy around people I don't know, but this was different.

Then, the ritual started and I felt so many wonderful emotions. I wanted to cry because I finally felt I was with those who knew what I was talking about, who felt basically how I felt. That weekend was so special to me. One of my favorite memories is of Acacia standing up in the wind driving the boat with her hair blowing wild and folk music playing on the tape deck. I may have seemed quiet to most of Copper Key, but I was very busy. I was watching all of them very closely and trying to soak in as much as I could because I didn't know if I would see any of them again. I was there as a guest. I was feeding off of their love. Ask Branwen—I talked of nothing else for weeks.

When she invited me to Circle with Copper Key again, I was thrilled! I knew I was home.

COMMITTING TO ADVENTURE

"RETREATS ARE important because the short times that we're to-gether for regular Circles, a couple of hours at a time, are real intensified ritual. Over two or three days you get to be more introspective and discuss things that you just can't discuss with anybody else," Orchid said after a Copper Key trip to the country in early 1993. "I sure can't talk to my husband about astral projection, and I don't have any other friends I can tell about my dreams or other things. Retreats keep you sane, and it's good bonding for the group. You get to discuss different viewpoints, and it helps you figure out your problems and also things about the Craft. It does for me anyway. I have thoughts bouncing around in my head, and until they come down and I speak them, I can't see them very clearly."

The decision to undertake a road trip must be made with full disclosure of the time, money, and energy involved for all parties. Space must be located and secured, deposits (if any) paid on cabins or campground, meals planned and supplies purchased, activities coordinated—and all this on top of planning for the central ritual. With so much to do, the group must be committed to making the trip a success and each member must be ready to contribute their time, talent, and dollars.

In an ideal situation, a member of the group will volunteer her own cabin or be able to secure one for free. More likely, a state park or private retreat center will be your destination. As many groups select Sabbats and holidays for travel, you may even find that your favorite location is booked—sometimes for the eight particular week-ends that you had in mind. Such was the case for Copper Key, and they later found out that another Coven had indeed reserved the retreat center on each Sabbat for the following two years.

Deposits vary from place to place, and depend upon the amount of space your group may require. Count on at least $100 for any indoor facility, less for campgrounds. Keep in mind that some members of your group may not be keen on tents; as with every other decision which will affect the group, discuss the options in advance. A realistic and practical timetable follows this section.

Retreats are ideal times to experiment, particularly if they are members only events. Some groups may find that the only time they are able to do work out of doors is when they pack up and head for a retreat site. "In our daily lives we can't always get out and be true to the Nature that we believe in," Hannah said. "In the city, it's harder to focus. On retreat, you're out under the sky, in the woods, you've got all that around you. It makes a difference." There may be specific aspects of the outdoors referenced in planned rituals, such as the throwing of eggs into water on Ostara, or casting the ashes of written vows onto a moving stream. Maybe walking through the woods at night with penlights to spot the eyes of tiny spiders appeals to your group, or being able to set a true bonfire over which to jump at Beltane. Trying new things for ritual, such as meditation or power-raising is best done when the group is meeting without guests.

Copper Key chose a retreat to leap into that part of Paganism which they had discussed (but not acted upon) for two years: meeting Skyclad. Some feel that the term is just a fancy word for naked and was probably added to the practice of the Old Religion in modern times; others say that it is indeed an authentic practice and that the Charge of the Goddess[1] specifically requires it. The women of Copper Key faced the question with the undeniable and inescapable baggage each of them had collected while living in today's modern world. Perhaps body image itself had more to do with their restraint than any other single factor. The retreat provided a place and a time away from the city and from strangers to face their fears head-on. Here's what they had to say:

---

[1] Prayer specifically addressing Witches and their practice of the Old Religion and worship of the Goddess; see page 90 of The Spiral Dance for Starhawk's translation/interpretation.

Author: So what about female body image? Is tonight the night you plan to do your first Skyclad ritual?

Orchid: It is too damn cold for me to do anything outside naked!

River: I have no problem with it as long as we do it indoors.

Ginger: We've been kind of leading up to this. We all went to a seminar on women's spirituality a month or so ago. One part of the day was a group ritual where, first of all, a group of women were drumming really well, not like the way we usually drum. Then this really large woman in a powder blue sweat suit with these huge tits and this big body and belly and hips and gray hair bursts into the middle of the circle, and she's moving up and down and her whole body moved with her in time to the drumming. It was like watching the ocean. Her breasts and belly would go up in the air and then come down in this tidal wave and you could really see the cycles of the Moon in her.

Orchid: It was beautiful.

Foxfire: It was just incredible.

Ginger: And I made eye contact with her, and then I came out from the side and danced with her and then there were two of us with these type bodies, and I could just feel the feminine power of it. You could feel pelvis. You could feel breasts. You could feel sweat.

Orchid: And there was another older woman, with that long, pretty skirt, and she was dancing along the sides—

Foxfire: She was dancing in a spiral —

Ginger: And this skirt was just ballooning out and she held her hands out to the group—

Orchid: And then she sort of went down into herself in that skirt, and then other people started dancing.

Foxfire: You could just see the energy between Ginger and the woman in the blue outfit, and the whole place seemed connected to them. It was unbelievable.

Orchid: There must have been six or seven of us there from Copper Key.

Foxfire: And we were like a big organic unit, people were noticing us as a definite group. They were watching us. It's like they could see the energy between us.

Ginger: And people were drawn to it.

Foxfire: And they came and even asked us about it.

Ginger: People were drawn to us and would move in to be part of it, and the group would split in half, like an amoeba, and join up again on the other side.

Foxfire: That's true. They weren't sure who we were, but they knew we were something.

Ginger: The only thing they could see there was the bond. I kept thinking people would figure out that this was the Coven. I'm out of the broom closet, they know I'm a Witch, and they know I'm in a Coven. But nobody made the connection. People said to me afterwards, "Was anyone else from your Coven there?"

Foxfire: Seriously, a lot of them never figured it out.

Ginger: I'm telling you, it's the boat in the harbor — you have to have a shaman to tell you how to see it.

Author: So that's what made you decide to try a meeting Skyclad?

Mer-Nuit: Well, I was reading *The God of the Witches*, by Margaret Murray, and I told the group the story about how some Witch two hundred or three hundred years ago had been on trial and part of the evidence against her was that she had gone running naked through the woods at night and had called out, "Robin, Robin, Robin," and that was the evidence that she was trying to call up the God. And I was thinking that's so different from what we do at Circle. We welcome the God in our Circle, but I think it's a whole different thing than maybe what our ancestors did. So I told the group about that story, and the next thing I hear is that we're all going to run around the woods on Friday night of the retreat naked, calling "Robin, Robin, Robin."

Ginger: From Mer-Nuit's story, I started thinking about things, and I guess I really am a mystic. I believe there is something out there. I believe the Horned God is out there.

River: I don't know if I would want a Horned God from this part of the country...

Foxfire: I need to run naked through the woods looking for Boudiccea!

Ginger: Who?

Foxfire: She was a Celtic sovereign. She led their troops and basically kicked the Romans' butts. They fought naked and painted themselves blue all over.

Ginger: Something about that women's festival made us think about celebrating women's bodies, and the bodies that *we* had. And I've been reading *Women Who Run With the Wolves*, and I hit the chapter on body image, and it is so interesting, Pinkola-Estes talks about her own personal experience, she says she's built close to the ground and wide, so I think I know what her body type is. She said her best friend is a very tall Black woman who is skinny and has a space between her teeth, and this woman was told as a child that if you had a space between your teeth it meant you were stupid and that men didn't like skinny women. And of course, the author grew up with a background that taught her that men like little petite skinny women. So, in their individual travels, the Black woman went back to Africa and literally found the tribe of her ancestry. She came into the village, and everybody there was tall and skinny, just like her. And a lot of them had the space between their teeth, and they told her that everyone would listen to people with that space, because it meant you were wise, even as a child. The author went to Mexico, where her ancestors came from, and the women there were concerned that she was too thin, and they told her she had to eat more, because women are round like the world. The fact is that your body size is a factor of genetics, and unless you torture yourself, there's not much you can do. And that body type is a message and a gift and it ought to be celebrated. It's not a fashion statement, this is sacred writing. This is where the ark is.

Orchid: So how do I get this message across to my daughter (Maroona) when she asks how much Cindy Crawford weighs?

Ginger: What you say is, what do you think Cindy Crawford's mother looks like? I think Maroona will choose a message, and it might not be the one you give her, but at least you are giving her an alternative to what she's going to see out there in the media.

Orchid: I think she's wrestling with it. I don't think she's totally swallowing the media message yet, but I know she is thinking about it really hard. You know, I told her to think about you, Ginger, and I hope you don't mind, but I asked her if she would love you more if you were real skinny like Cindy Crawford. And she said, "No." And I asked her if she would want you to be any other way than what you are right now, and she said no. I also asked her how things would change or be better for her if I could make her skinny just like that. She didn't have an answer. But she's already worried about boys liking her. Some of the girls in her class are already growing tall and maturing, and she thinks she's going to be a chubby little kid all her life. I've got a two-inch figure of the Venus of Willendorf. I showed it to her and told her that this is the image of the Goddess and that before Christianity this is the figure that everybody worshiped. Do you see how fat this woman is, her big breasts and belly? They thought this was the ideal woman, this image was sacred. Now, is this woman skinny? No.

Ginger: Looks don't really matter to men in the long run anyway. They are attracted to nurturing, warmth, aliveness, vivaciousness, and that's all that counts. I dated a photographer and it was really hard, because he spent all day with models, with beautiful women, and they all adored him. I couldn't understand why he chose me over them. But he told me that every single one of them had hangups and problems and he photographed them all day and that was enough for him.

Acacia: And what about the women who go out of their way to look like that? Did you know that women who get breast implants generally lose all sensation in their nipples?

River: Nine times out of ten, all feeling is lost, that's right.

Acacia: So they are giving up part of their sexual identity and sexual sensation to have bigger boobs.

Orchid: Can you imagine not being able to feel your own breasts?

Ginger: If I had to have a mastectomy, that's one of the things I would really mourn the loss of, the sensuality of it.

Hannah: That's true, not just the mutilation and the loss of that tissue but also the loss of feeling.

Acacia: And I have also talked with women who have had breast reduction, and the same loss of sensation is usually there. Of course their decision is generally based on the fact that they have some physical problem because of the weight of their breasts. It's a difficult thing. But I saw on TV a group of exotic dancers who had had enlargement surgery, and they were asked about it, and they all said they'd just as soon give up that sensation to have men like them.

Hannah: How much time do they spend with a man anyway? Other than sleeping with them, are they spending 24 hours a day caring about what men think about their breasts?

River: Some people are desperate for any attention from men.

Acacia: What happens when they turn sixty-five, and their husbands or whoever are aging, and they are still mutilated — they won't be able to get that sensation back.

River: I can't imagine taking a knife to my body just so somebody else will like it. Forget it.

Ginger: From someone who has big tits, let me tell you, men who are enamored of them are so fixated that the person might as well not even be there.

Orchid: Sometimes I wonder if they're not just a hindrance to relationships. I've got this friend with a Marilyn Monroe figure, and she complains all the time about men. She says when they have sex, they don't ever want to do anything else but play with her breasts.

Ginger: If men focus on any one part of your body to the exclusion of the rest of you, you become essentially just parts. There's more to me—there's a whole body, knees, legs, hair, ears, cunt, neck, eyes—

Hannah: We are whole beings, not just pieces.

Ginger: And inside of those parts is a whole human soul.

Orchid: I remember the first girl that developed in my class, and she got big breasts all in one year. All the boys wanted to sit next to her on the bus and poke her in the chest and go steady with her so they could feel her breasts.

Hannah: That happened to me. I had little boys come up and pinch my nipples—we were the same age, but it was horrible to go through.

The weather was, indeed, much colder than had been predicted for this particular retreat. Whether that played a part in their decision to wait just one more night to go skyclad or not is debatable; however, they did take the jump the very next evening.

Owing to the continued cold weather, the group voted to go bare-chested rather than completely naked. In keeping with the idea of honoring their bodies and their ancestors, Ginger brought along body paints. The women took turns painting each other's faces, necks, fronts, and backs with symbols derived from many different cultures: Orchid's Native American heritage was honored by the war paint across her cheeks and forehead; Acacia wore a double crescent pattern on her throat that she found in information about her Italian Craft cousins; River painted Celtic knots and a chalice across her chest. Hannah crafted spirals and spiders and triangles and moons and other symbols on everyone's cheeks, and each person had a blue Shaman's hand on her back.

It was not all gung-ho baring of breasts, to be sure. More than one member sat back and waited until almost the last moment to undress. Those women who had participated in Skyclad ceremonies before were much more confident than those who had never attended one. But there was not any goading or snickering to convince these women to participate; every single person who attended the retreat knew well in advance of the plans, and had any one of them decided not to go through with it, she would have taken her place in the Circle regardless. In fact, Ivy had brought her newborn along on the trip and was breast-feeding; going without support became very uncomfortable for her and she got dressed when she felt the need. As with so many other things in your Craft community life, if anyone is not ready to take a step such as this, give it some time rather than press the issue.

After donning their decoration next to the fireplace in the cabin, the women proceeded outside to the ritual area. There was not a fire ring nearby, so they took along jackets and sweaters. Once outside, the "spirit" moved several members who went ahead and dropped the last of their clothes and participated in the New Moon Ceremony completely Skyclad. It is interesting to note that the two women who lasted the longest without cover were both over forty-five.

A retreat in and of itself is likely to produce unexpected behavior, both good and bad. The good things you can learn are endless; you might not know that one of the women in your Circle can name each and every flower and plant in the region, or that another might be able to tell you what animal has been sniffing around your campsite by the tracks. But be prepared to find out who snores, who hates to do dishes, who is likely to get lost even when they have a map, and who might not be able to stand creepy-crawlies.

Of course, personal safety must always be the first item on your agenda. You might find yourself facing problems which you may not feel ready to handle. Make it clear up front that each person is responsible for her own behavior and her actions while on the road, and that consideration for the group should govern both.

Alcohol and controlled substances are another issue which should be addressed before leaving for the country. Make a point to find out about regulations in the area in which you will be traveling; most state parks are alcohol-free environments, and you may also find yourself traveling through a dry county to get to your destination. Remember that consideration for the group means that if one person is uncomfortable, the group should make other plans. (An individual who wishes to imbibe must take the feelings of her Circle into account.)

PRACTICAL PLANNING OUTLINE

SCHEDULE

Three+ months prior:
- Set a date and get commitments; decide whether significant others and children or guests are to be included.
- Assign a Scouting Party to locate a site.
- Assign Priestesses for the ritual(s).

Two+ months prior:
- Assign two or more to plan activities.
- Discuss meals—select a Meals Chairperson.
- Scouting Party report—vote on possible locations.
- Collect money for deposit—firm up your head-count, and decide how to handle "backouts" (refund money? etc.).
- Discuss transportation.

One month prior:
- Activities report—let group know what they need to bring
- Meals Chair report—firm up commitments to bring items and to cook
- Discuss alcohol/drugs group policy
- Discuss behavior of guests (if any); decide if guests will take part in ritual(s), and be certain that each member bringing guests has ex-

	plained the nature and content of the upcoming trip.[1]
	• Assign a Phone Chair to make reminder calls and to be certain everyone has transportation.
One week prior:	• Phone Chair makes first set of reminder calls.
	• Priestess firms up commitments from members to help with parts of the ritual(s).
	• Meals Chair makes reminder calls.
Day before:	• Phone Chair makes final reminder calls.
Day of the retreat:	• Members meet at previously designated starting point and caravan to the retreat site.

RESPONSIBILITIES

Scouting Party: At least two people should volunteer to undertake the task of finding places suitable for the group to visit. Suggestions: state and national parks in the area; retreat centers recommended by your women's bookstore; private land to which a member of the group has access. Commercial campgrounds are risky—a member of the Scouting Party should check one campground out in person to be sure there are areas private enough for ritual and activities before committing to it. In fact, where possible, Scouts should make the drive to all possible sites to check on security, space, and local amenities (restaurants, grocery stores, etc.). If getting out of town is impossible, Scouts might check the local YWCA for meeting rooms, or even meeting rooms at local hotels and motels which can be reserved for the day. If the weather is too cold or too hot for outside accommodations, see what's in the vicinity in the way of bed-and-breakfasts that are Pagan-friendly

---

[1] See "Possible Pitfalls," Chapter VII.

(check *Ferrari's Places for Women*), or even check into a hotel with adjoining rooms. Scouts should consciously look for places which will cause the least amount of friction for the group—while making a stand on the right to assembly and freedom of religion is, of course, important for the future safety of alternative groups, it might not be conducive to group bonding and religious experience. One member of the Scouts should plan to serve as temporary treasurer for the collection and disbursement of any money needed for deposits, rental fees, etc.

Priestesses: As with any ritual you plan, the altar may be elaborate or simple, the decorations intricate or basic, the work of the Circle lengthy or abbreviated. It is the choice of the Priestesses. You may decide not to take any but the most essential altar tools (source candle, wand, athame) and improvise the rest with found objects from the area where the retreat is being held—even if it's at the Holiday Inn: stationery for an altar cloth, complimentary pen or pencil for a staff, pillow chocolates for Cakes, a soap cake to honor Air (smell), a beverage glass to mix water and salt (from a packet you lifted at the restaurant downstairs), and unlimited fluffy towels for each member following the ritual bath. Be creative, and you might not have to haul your living room with you. Of course, it is always a treat when you are camping and out of someone's car comes all the decor appropriate to the holiday. Just remember that you are not the Lone Ranger and that asking for help is not only a good idea but is probably expected.

Activities Chairs: Featuring the skills and knowledge of particular members for activities is smart planning. Tara, among her other talents, happened to be adept at leading past life regression meditations, and a time was cleared on the weekend's agenda for her to work with the group. Laurel brought along intuition games to play on one retreat, and Acacia planned a cleanup session for the lake on which they stayed at another. You may take your cue from the time of year, the Sabbat mythology (i.e., dancing the Maypole for Beltane), the location, or the projects with which your group might already be involved. A retreat might be a good time to finish sewing the details onto robes, or making candles for everyone's altars, or locating items for personal shrines, or making Fimo images of the Goddess. Find out who knows about the stars and plan a session of stargazing. Look for divination tools which the group might begin mastering. Have everyone come ready to tell a story from the pantheon with which they like to work. Think back on activities which you liked as a child — they are probably just perfect for your Coven. Play games like hide-and-seek. More than likely, you will have more activities planned than time; just don't ride the group or yourself too hard if not every activity comes off without a hitch. (Some suggested group activities can be found in Appendix 1).

Meals Chair: This job will not be as hard as you might think at the outset. No one expects this person to do the meal plans, grocery shopping, cooking and cleaning — rather, the Meals Chair will help the group decide how meals will be handled: pot luck; teams to do breakfasts, lunches, and dinners; group contributions; a team of shoppers; local restaurants; or a combination of any of the above. The Meals Chair should also help the group decide if sticking to seasonally appropriate meals will work out for the weekend (i.e., Thanksgiving feast at Mabon, pickled foods and first harvest items at Lammas, etc.). The meals chair should also lead the discussion on dietary practices (chances are at least one member of your group will not be an omnivore). Some members may have food allergies that need to be addressed. If guests are to be included in the retreat, the group should decide if they will be responsible for helping with meals, too. This person should work closely with the Scouting Party to find out what facilities are available for preparing meals, or if it will be more time efficient and cost-effective to plan for some meals at local restaurants.

Phone Chair: This person must check and double check that she has the information from all the above parties correct before she begins calling to remind everyone what they need to bring, where they need to meet or pick up maps, the attire for the weekend, items for planned activities, the estimated amount of money for any meals, etc. Should she need to leave messages on answering machines, she should ask that the member call her back to confirm that the message was received. While it can be quite complicated to initiate, this person might decide to design a "phone tree" for the Coven, where she distributes the list of names and numbers of all the Coven to the group, and then, when a message needs to get to everyone, calls the person at the beginning and the person at the end, whose job it is to call the person listed above and below their own names. The next person calls both the person above and below their own name, and so on. This generally assures that everyone gets the message at least once, although for complex instructions, the phone chair might feel more comfortable knowing she had personally spoken to every member. Again, whatever works for your group is what works, period.

Troubleshooting: The Priestess might assign a Challenger for the ritual (as described in *Elements of Copper Key Rituals*). On a retreat, if this person is willing, she might also serve as the watchdog[2] for the weekend and be the designated individual to administer first aid, get help from the local fire department or police if needed, and know how to find the closest hospital or ranger station. If your group designates such an individual, it must be made clear at the outset that she is the person to whom to defer in an emergency—she should be well prepared and ready at a moment's notice to get help if any unforeseen situation should arise. Even when everyone is being their most careful, accidents can happen. It is always best to have someone on duty who has planned ahead and can be calm and focused to take care of the problem.

Even with all the work and careful planning needed to make a success out of a group retreat, the benefits far outweigh the costs. It might be helpful to make a list of goals that your group as a whole or you as an individual wish to accomplish over a given retreat; at the first regular meeting following a retreat, be sure to leave time for discussing the things that worked and the things which need to be improved upon before the next adventure.

---

[2] While the Scouts have hopefully found a Pagan-safe place to meet, one never knows what to expect—at least one member of the group should be reasonably aware and alert to the possibility of strangers wandering into the campsite.

PAGAN FESTIVALS & GATHERINGS

IF YOU have been studying the Craft it won't be long before someone will introduce you to the idea of attending a Pagan Gatheringthese festivals occur all over the United States—and some Pagans even follow the entire festival route from late Spring through the Fall. There are gatherings for every possible taste, from strictly women only to strictly gay men and their friends, and everything in between. Some celebrate specific events in the Wheel of the Year like particular holidays, while some gather to celebrate the general Pagan experience. The idea of spending a few days in a remote area with hundreds of people who worship the way you do is indeed alluring; there is even a certain mystique which promotes the festival circuit without anyone spending a dime on advertising. But like everything else in life, asking the necessary questions about the gathering will probably save you from being disappointed.

"Before my first gathering, I thought it was going to be like Young Life camp," Laurel said. "It was just going to be *so* moving and *so* wonderful, it was going to change my life, and I was going to come home knowing everything anyone could ever learn at such a workshop, and everyone there was going to be so wonderful, open, and loving—one big happy Pagan community. Reality quickly set in. First, it was very disorganized, and very egocentric—a large gathering of more than 250 people, only honoring the egos of a few. The facilities were abysmal—people who camped had to deal with a muddy parking lot on which to pitch tents; very little water; toilets in the woods, very few communal showers. Obviously, I'm not the type of person who is cut out for a Pagan gathering, although I still occasionally get the urge to go."

Attending a Pagan gathering for the first time can be an over-whelming experience. You may have a hard time connecting with the throng of people, and you may not be sure about proper etiquette. There will probably be a very relaxed idea of proper attire (as little as possible, or none at some festivals); men may be running around with tiny plastic antlers fixed to their scalps; you probably won't be able to pick out the accountant or the schoolteacher or the lawyer in the bunch. Gatherings tend to be a little like fantasy camp; there are few expectations for personal conduct, and anything goes. So what's the draw, you may be wondering?

Acacia reported, "There were seminars all day both Friday and Saturday, led by names I recognized from the books I had been reading about the Craft, like Janet and Stewart Farrar. A marketplace was set up for Pagan artists to sell their wares, a lot of things you don't see in the stores. And everyone there was Pagan and comfortable as a Pagan. It was *no big deal to be different*—I felt as if I was finally immersed in a whole village that understood. I didn't have to hide my religious beliefs. It's a real shame it was only for a weekend."

Copper Key has sent delegations to different Pagan gatherings around the country. River and Branwen, who attended the Pagan Spirit Gathering (PSG) in Wisconsin, report that it is one of the better-run events. It is held for a week around Summer Solstice. It has a reputation for being an intense, focused week of spiritual growth; in fact, the organizers, Circle Sanctuary, dedicate an entire area of the gathering ground as a "retreat space" so that people can take a break from the concentrated effort the workshops and seminars require. "The fact that you're there for a whole week makes a difference," River said. "When you leave, you wish that the world could be as open and understanding as PSG. I try to go every year."

Acacia and Laurel both attended the first Gathering of the Tribes, sponsored by the Church of Y Tylwyth Teg, Inc. "There were some fairly good workshops, and I met some really interesting people, like Brie Foxsong, Isaac Bonewits, Otter Zell, some others," Laurel said. "I would say Gathering of the Tribes is one gathering to consider attending. I was more comfortable there because everyone remained clothed. I took my dedication to Hidden Grove there."

"My first gathering was sponsored by Green Egg and the Church of All Worlds, and the theme for the weekend was Greek ritual," Mer-Nuit said. "The one thing I was not prepared for was the casual attitude toward nudity—it was a different world to me. We were in a public place, a university athletic field. The men who were competing in some Olympic-style games were wearing loincloths; some fell off. Everyone just laughed. And the men finished whatever they were doing nude."

Ginger also attended the gathering. "I didn't feel sexually threatened—of course, I didn't take off my clothes, but I think I might be ready to tackle it at my next Pagan festival. I was surprised that I found public ritual so meaningful with people whom I didn't know. The weekend was well planned, and parts of the ritual and the dancing were just breathtaking. "

"I would probably go to another one, although some are too expensive," Mer-Nuit added, "but I am hoping our local Women's Spirituality Festival will grow."

If you are uncertain about trekking to a campground or driving to a distant city to attend a gathering or festival, check close to home first. In the area near Copper Key, there were more than a dozen gatherings, spirituality festivals, seminars, weekends, and classes in less than a year. One was led by Starhawk and the Reclaiming Collective. She taught and shared ritual with a group of one hundred or more women at the local college. You might even use your list of contacts—bookstores, universities, Unitarian churches, National Organization for Women chapters—to organize a gathering of your own or to invite a speaker like Starhawk to visit your community.

Should you decide to attend an open meeting of any kind, here are some things to remember:

- Make sure that you are not signing a consent to be identified by the press at the event if you are not out of the broom closet. Some events will have media coverage. A photographer from Time Magazine snapped a few shots of Ginger & Mer-Nuit at the gathering they discussed above, and another member of Copper Key ended up in a photo accompanying a news article about a gathering she attended although she had not signed any agreement giving the journalist permission to use her likeness—the staff of the gathering had given the reporter permission to cover the event.

- If you are approached by a reporter at an open meeting, don't assume that because he or she seems to "walk the walk and talk the talk" he or she will understand your need for anonymity and won't identify you in a news story—discuss the terms under which you are willing to talk to the media before the interview.

- Almost every gathering you attend will require that you register under your legal name for insurance purposes; they will also require home address and phone number. What they do with this information later may be of concern—Laurel was contacted by a police officer who was looking for a speaker at one of his seminars on alternative religions because her name had been given to him by the group which sponsored a gathering she had attended.

- Most organized Pagan gatherings will cost between $100-$400 to attend, including space in which to camp. Others may allow you to barter or do a work-exchange to cover your registration fee. In addition, take into account the cost of traveling to the event, meals (if they are not included), and a budget for spending money in the marketplace.

- Plan to be open-minded and put your preconceived ideas away for the weekend; you and your group will be exposed to so many different ways of doing things it is impossible to be prepared for them all.

JOURNAL ENTRIES

1. When I think about spending two or three days alone with a group, I have hopes and I have reservations. They are:

2. If I am asked to volunteer to be responsible for something on a retreat, this is what I think I could do successfully:

3. Before our first retreat, this is how I feel:

4. How did I feel the first night home from retreat? What one thing would I want to see added to the next retreat.

5. These retreat activities were satisfying/not satisfying for me:

6. How would I feel spending time at a Pagan gathering with people from all over the country? How comfortable am I mixing in with different groups?

7. How do I feel about meeting Skyclad? If I had been a member of Copper Key the night they first tried it, I would have:

COPPER KEY RECOMMENDS:

The Beauty Myth, by Naomi Wolf; New York: Doubleday, ©1991.

The God of the Witches, by Margaret Murray; New York: Oxford University Press, ©1970.

Ferrari's Places For Women, by Marianne Ferrari, ed.; Phoenix: Ferrari Publications, Inc., ©1993 (published annually).

Women Who Run With the Wolves, by Clarissa Pinkola Estés, Ph.D.;
New York: Ballantine Books, ©1992.

For an Annual List of Pagan Gatherings, contact:
Circle Sanctuary
Box 219
Mt. Horeb, Wisconsin 53572

7
GROUP DYNAMICS WITHIN THE SPIRAL

GINGER'S STORY

MY STORY is one of remembering the choreography, feeling the soulful rhythm of the Moon, the tide, Earth, passion, Air, Fire, and Water. I am all things, all things are me.

In retrospect, there were always Pagan signs. My earliest memories include the ability to drift away from any unpleasant situation. I could always go back to seeing my grandmother's steamy kitchen where homegrown vegetables were canned at the end of each summer. I could gaze at light on the walls and "leave"—reaching for heat and light when I was trapped in cold and darkness.

I remember crawling behind the rambling rose bush and shrinking down, pretending to grow wings and live as a solitary fairy princess with a magic sword. But such fanciful stories were in short supply in my solid Methodist home, where the holy word of science was carefully reconciled with biblical doctrine. Fairy tales were thought too frightening for a child, but the theory of photosynthesis lent explanations to the magic of magnolia trees.

My parents openly proclaimed to me that they went to church only to set an example for me. I marveled at adults groveling before an invisible "Father," begging for mercy. What? Saved? I didn't want to be saved by a daddy, I wanted to be safe from them, by flight on fairy wing, or just hurrying to be grown-up myself.

The woods were always best—my grandfather was a game ranger, and he showed me a pair of gray wolves once, saying, "I want you to see this, because your children will never see these wolves." He was right—they are extinct in the Kinishia Mountains now. He taught me that wild animals are always wild and should not be kept in fences. Now I know that hearts are wild, too, and should not be kept in cages.

The spirituality I felt in the woods and the exhilaration of running screaming down a hill had no name for years and remained apart from the rest of my life. I professed to find Jesus at twelve, I married in a small chapel at eighteen, and I divorced in a courtroom a decade later after Betty Friedan advised me, ". . . don't iron while the strike is hot— get a college degree."

So I did. Divorced and with two daughters, I became an entering freshman at 27. My world expanded exponentially. I learned to dissect a fetal pig; I read anthropology and poetry; I could expound on economic theory so well I made the Dean's List. I also learned it was important to see what went bump in the night; it was a time of profound courage and exploration. I read Kate Millet's *Sexual Politics*, and met Gloria Steinem at a rally. I was one of five organized feminists on our tiny college campus—we formed a Consciousness Raising Group and discussed what female eroticism would be without male symbolism. I learned to ask a man for a date and how to get a job.

It was during this period that I fell in with a fundamental, charismatic Christian community. It was a truly joyful group of people who had splintered off from a Church of Christ congregation because of their theological interpretation of the Adam and Eve story—they held Adam equally culpable for the Fall since he took the apple from Eve. Encouraged by this radical feminist view, I literally dove into those baptismal waters. The group provided a sense of community; we fasted on Sundays til the evening when there was a wonderful potluck dinner, preceded and followed by Bible study. The myth and stories intrigued me: flaming chariots rising to the heavens, David dancing for joy naked before the Ark of the Covenant, and Jesus telling stories to an enraptured Mary (of the Mary and Martha duo), who washed his feet with her hair. That last story proved to be my undoing.

For those of you who are unfamiliar with the story, let me summarize: Jesus was wandering around the Middle East when he was called to go to the home of his friend, Lazarus. (Scripture is silent on how he was called in the desert; no messenger is mentioned— telepathy?) He arrives at the destination and raises Lazarus' decaying corpse from the tomb. Jesus stays to enjoy a feast with the family, prepared by the sisters of Lazarus, Mary and Martha. While Martha is in the kitchen cooking, Mary is in the parlor washing Jesus' feet and drying them with her hair.

This story was the topic of discussion one evening, with the focus on raising the dead. I was much more enticed by the relationship between Jesus and this particular Mary. When I asked if there were other biblical references to Jesus' lovers, there was a collective gasp of horror. How could I possibly conclude that Jesus was a sexual being? "If I washed a man's feet and dried them with my hair, I guarantee he'd be getting laid." In addition to getting some insight into institutional Christianity's view of sexuality, I gained a profound sense of the nature of blasphemy. After an extensive discussion of these issues, I left, never to call myself Christian again, but I had nevertheless been baptized by living waters into community and the sweet honey of myth.

During this same period, an incident occurred that was one of those signals that I would recognize later. One afternoon, I was overcome with the need for sleep, not uncommon for a student working two jobs and managing a family. I left class and hurried home; I had only two hours before I was to pick up my youngest daughter from daycare. I staggered into the apartment and headed down the hall toward the bedroom. I heard a roar of water and I imagined a waterfall, but dismissed the idea. Then my bare feet hit soaking wet carpet. Had the hot water heater broken? Exhausted, I fell to my knees; water soaked through the legs of my Levis. There was water everywhere. Then the roar of gushing water diminished and a voice said, "For behold, I have been with you from the beginning." I could not open my eyes; I crawled to the bed and collapsed. I awoke an hour later, in bone-dry jeans. The carpet was dry, the hot water heater was intact. Two decades later, I would hear those words as the Charge of the Goddess was recited. And the voice in my apartment and the voice in the ritual were both female.

After graduation from college, I was busy with my career, raising my daughters, feminism, and the single life. I joined the Unitarian Church, because it not only offered the hottest singles group in town and volleyball, but also the classic UU inquiry, careful intellectual exploration with the highest spirit of rationalism. However sterile and coolly introspective the process, it was the beginning of an examined life. Later that examined life included an extensive period of psycho-therapy where I reclaimed my childhood. I had to face the issue of suffering—why do bad things happen? In painful step by painful step, I faced my hidden memories and began to understand abuse and finally began the healing process. Letting go of my denial included facing the reality that my family life was not like "Ozzie & Harriet." I recognized that I was never going to have a loving father. I was never able to visualize a solitary, loving, invisible Father, either. Christianity would never be acceptable again. However, the mystic healing of the woods, the light of the Moon, and the changing seasons still stirred me deeply and brought a sense of wholeness.

In my late forties, I began a conscious, focused search. I met a profoundly loving and holy woman, Sister Anne, who gave me language for this mysticism—words like ecstasy and pantheism. She introduced me to the theology of Father Matthew Fox, Thomas Merton, Julian, and Hildegaard of Beghium. For the first (and to date only) time, Christianity was presented to me without rancor, without expectation of conversion, and with a profound sense of respect for my own experience and intrinsic value. Sister Anne belongs to an order of Sisters who see poverty as oppression and who make a connection between violence of spirit and war. (If Christianity ever goes back to its 12th Century roots, it'll give Paganism a run for its money.) Anne shared with me ideas about living in community, and the need for and the power of ritual. We had many careful, thoughtful discussions, and with her help I began to form my own cosmology: I believe in a web of life in which both mortals and Divinities exist. How could I dismiss the Elements?

The next major event in recognizing my Path was participating in a twelve-week course called "Cakes for the Queen of Heaven." The Cakes curriculum (still available at your local Unitarian Universalist Church) introduces feminist spirituality, including Goddess art, re-written myths, and, most enticing for me, the eighth session on Witchcraft. Of the twelve women in our "Cakes" group, one did not finish the course because it threatened her Christian faith; eight remained Unitarians; three of us are now on a Wiccan path. None of the succeeding five groups studying the curriculum produced a single Witch; I believe Witches are drawn together and to the Path.

The eighth session on Witchcraft offered in this course includes a discussion of the burning times with a simple candle-lighting ritual. Our group elected to expand this discussion and to have a potluck at the UU church. Elizabeth dressed as a "witch" (all in black) and built a small fire in a barbecue grill; we gathered around it for the ritual. Since none of us knew anything about Wicca or Witchcraft other than the general description in the curriculum, we ended up around a campfire laughing at ourselves. Cast a Circle? I don't think any of us even knew that phrase, but we were a circle of friends. We felt that music was necessary, so one of the women brought her guitar. The only women's songs we knew were Girl Scout songs. It was a start.

Our Cakes group continued to meet after we completed the curriculum. One of the alternative activities of the Witchcraft section was to go ask a local Witch to conduct a Wiccan circle. One of our members did in fact know a local Witch, whom we invited to do a ritual for us. Her name is EarthWalker; she is in her sixties and practices with a women's Moon Lodge.

We met on a Sunday afternoon in July at Laura's house. EarthWalker arrived with coffee cans for drums and her own candles. She is a small, slender woman with white hair who lives out in the country with her husband. She explained a few basic principles: men ruin the energy and they shouldn't be at or near the ritual if possible; whoever is Priestessing decides on the ritual; old age, and old women in particular, are honored. She told us we couldn't make a mistake. We nodded gravely, promising to note all the details and do it right. "No, no, when I said you can't make a mistake, I mean there are no mistakes. Whatever you do is RIGHT." For a group of highly-motivated superwomen with careers, it was a new notion. I am still dealing with it.

After this orientation, we began by lining up single file with the oldest at the head. "My religion honors age," EarthWalker said. Women should never be ashamed of their age. They should tell their age with pride. Then EarthWalker led us in a spiral procession, cutting a psychic path with a kitchen knife. There we were, a bunch of middle-aged women chanting and singing and tramping around a suburban front yard led by a woman wielding a butcher knife. While it seemed the most reasonable activity in the sweet universe to us, it is one of those things that could be misinterpreted by the mundane world as either threatening or ridiculous. We went into the living room, sat in a Circle, lit candles, invited the Goddess to join us, and drummed and chanted our joyful little hearts out. I was charmed in every sense of the word.

Mer-Nuit and I began to look around the community for a group. I didn't have a specific idea of what a Pagan group would be, but I tend to look for an expert, take a class, or get certified at whatever I do. So that was my unconscious mode of operation at this spiritual quest as well. Mer-Nuit is an anthropologist, so she began researching Paganism. After several months, neither of us was successful, but I think we unwittingly put out a "Coven Call."

She and I decided to form our own group at the UU church. As a member, I could reserve one of the rooms for a meeting and put an announcement in the church newsletter. At the first meeting, about five women showed up for our "earth-centered spirituality" study group, including a church board member and the head of religious education. We talked about wanting to study the Web and Nature ideas. The religious education director said, "Oh, we do that for the children; here are the books—it's innocuous enough." Then she and the board member left. We should have been paying attention to their leaving, but it was not our focus. No one there, including us, really had any clear idea what we sought or how to become a group, and the meeting was dry and unsatisfying. Perhaps, we decided, if we went outdoors and did ritual, something would happen. What? I don't know. It just had to be better than this.

The second meeting was held outside on the church lawn at sunset. It was late summer and so beautiful; I wanted to dance, I was so happy. I was really insensitive to the dynamics of the group. I did not allow the others to look at the issues that had brought me to this point. It felt like the beginning to me, but in fact I had spent a year in searching, and that process is significant. I was surprised that sitting in a circle for ritual alarmed the others—it did. They would not even form a circle; they sat clustered together saying how they had to fit into the community and could not be different. Mer-Nuit and I sat away from the group and just looked at the sunset. We seemed to be getting nowhere.

Then, around the North side of the building came two women. "Hi, we heard you were having some king of ritual." "We were," I said, "but take a look. It's not working out." We chatted for a few minutes, then one of the women said, "Look!" I turned to the South and saw a fox—she was about ten feet away from us, looking directly into our eyes. I held my breath. The cluster of other women did not even stop talking—they did not even see it. Suddenly, the fox darted across the lawn to the edge of the woods, and then stood up on her hind legs to chase fireflies—she truly danced! My throat still closes and tears still rise remembering the perfection of that moment, that dance.

When the fox had disappeared into the woods, the two women told us they met with some other women at a bookstore in town and invited us to join them there. Incidentally, one of them took Foxfire as her Pagan name—it was the third time she had seen a fox up close in as many days.

I went to the next New Moon. Mer-Nuit and Hecate (from the Cakes group) went, too. The scene is still vivid in my mind—the bookstore was closed, but the door was open; all the women were milling around, some moving bookshelves out of the way. There were several conversations taking place simultaneously about every possible topic—natal charts to a squabble in the NOW chapter—and another group was gathered about a round cloth in the middle of the floor, debating which way was East and where to place the small potted plant on the "altar" cloth. My indestructible Girl Scout sense of direction leapt forward; "That way is North and that way is East," I said. "Are you sure?" grinned a pretty woman named Laurel, who was sitting on the floor supervising the arrangement of an odd assortment of objects on the cloth. She was bringing out candles, incense holders, a letter opener, a dish of salt, shells . . . When was this Mary Poppins going to pull out "eye of gnat"? There was a three-ring binder with file separators on the other side, and a massive file-o-fax. Good grief, a Witch with a file-o-fax! There must have been fifteen or so women, running the gamut of age, looks, and place in society. One was a young girl with a pierced nose wearing an Indian print skirt and combat boots—she was friendly and comforting, because my daughter had a friend with that look in high school, so it seemed, well, normal.

I was glad the two women were there who had invited me. I sat down on the floor for my first Wiccan Circle. It was a blur of lighting candles, singing unfamiliar songs, handing incense and water around. Everyone introduced themselves by Pagan names for security reasons, whatever that meant. Everyone was warm and friendly, there was a lot of laughter. One woman explained, "We are serious, we just don't take ourselves too seriously." Okay. Laurel walked around the Circle with a stick and cast the Circle. Uh-huh. We invited in the Directions and the Goddess and the God. I had read Starhawk, and although *Dreaming the Dark* didn't give a lot of details, this seemed in the spirit of the thing. I was overwhelmed . . . be careful what you wish for, for you will surely get it.

After the Circle, Mer-Nuit and I talked in the parking lot of the bookstore. She was thrilled and pronounced the event "very witchy." I thought the women were crazy. It just wasn't for me. But as the next New Moon approached, I was restless and decided to go again. This time the scene did not seem quite so strange. And again, Mer-Nuit and Hecate were there. As odd as the ritual was, the women were so warm, and they seemed like family. Again no one could remember which way was East. I relaxed a little, but it was still not my cup of tea.

Because I had been to two New Moons, I was invited to attend a Full Moon ceremony at one of the members' homes. I took the address down, and two weeks later found myself standing on a center-city porch under the Full Moon. There were flower pots filled with herbs, some of which I recognized. One was garlic—I thought, at least there wouldn't be vampires. If they serve Koolaid, I'll just pass. I knocked on the door. "Come in quickly, don't let the cats out!"

It was a smaller group than the open meetings at the bookstore; it was comforting to know that no one knew which way was East here, either. Gods! I loved these women. We moved the futon couch to the side of the room, creating an open space for the altar to be set up. I helped put the objects on the altar under Laurel's supervision. We all talked. I should note that by this time I knew something of their "regular" lives—they were artists, teachers, lawyers, business women, museum curators, and students (note their biographical surveys at the end of this book). But they were, above all, caring and responsible women. These Circles included not only candle-lighting and chanting, but also such practical things as arranging funds for one of the younger women (a student without medical insurance) to see a gynecologist, and networking about jobs and community projects. The checklist for cults in *Drawing Down the Moon*[1] yielded a resounding "Safe" signal. This stuff just sang to me!

After the Full Moon at Brahwen's which included a House Blessing, I was eligible to attend a Sabbat. I was invited up to a lake house a few hours East of town—I wondered if the group would find it, considering the collective lack of a sense of direction. Hecate and I decided to go. It was Mabon, the traditional time of the year for calling the Pagans home. It was on that retreat I blithely asked the group, "You don't really believe this, do you? I mean literally?"

The question was, did I believe?

---

[1] Isaac Bonewit's "Cult Danger Evaluation Frame," as reprinted in *Drawing Down the Moon,* page 509.

MY MAGIC OR YOURS?

THROUGHOUT THE Pagan world, debates rage on and on about who is "doing it right." One may overhear Druids arguing with Wiccans about women's roles in ritual, or one may run across a nasty note in a newsletter about Europeans' use of Native American smudge sticks. Occasionally, a good bit of prejudice is exposed in the discussion on which continent, country, or community actually worships the Gods the way they *should* be worshipped. And quite often at Pagan gatherings, Witchy one-upsmanship leaves an observer with the impression that even in supposedly spiritual environments, cliques are the order of the day.

Copper Key was originally comprised of many women who were on the verge of discovering what they truly believed in, not only as a group but also as individuals. Each brought to Circle ideas, research, ritual scripts, activities, and games from a wide range of sources, including popular fiction, archaeological surveys, and teaching materials from one or another Pagan Tradition. Early on, this eclectic mix of pantheons and magic was like a terrific smorgasbord; however, as time went on, members began to pick and choose the things that worked best for them as a Circle, the things which "sang" to them as a group, and also those things which seemed to call to them as individuals.

The greatest difficulty for Copper Key arose over some members' involvement with Hidden Grove, a national group that had students all over the country (it has since evolved into at least three groups nationwide). Clashes occurred over the following:

- Hidden Grove and its High Priestess and High Priest were often the subject of disagreement within Copper Key; the two groups were governed in completely opposite ways. Copper Key was an open democracy of sorts, whereas Hidden Grove was strictly ruled by its two founders. This was a sore point for the interaction of the women who participated in both groups with the women who participated solely in Copper Key.
- Students of Hidden Grove were required to commit their time to studying that tradition, as well as to meeting with other students in the area on the Lunar events and Sabbats. As the rituals of Copper Key were eclectic, members in both groups also had to attend a Hidden Grove ritual to meet the requirements of the teachers. This meant making time to attend two meetings for each New Moon, Full Moon, and Sabbat. Scheduling conflicts often caused tension in Copper Key, particularly when not all of Copper Key was studying with Hidden Grove. At one point, Copper Key even dropped New Moons in an attempt to allow the Hidden Grove students one meeting a month which would not be in conflict with Copper Key.
- Because of the involvement of at least five women of Copper Key with Hidden Grove, the rituals inside Copper Key began to take on the flavor of the teachings of the Hidden Grove tradition. For the women who chose not to study with Hidden Grove, this was often a disturbing addition.

If your own group decides to work with teachers from other traditions, it may be important to discuss the possible conflicts well in advance and to determine then and there the priorities for everyone involved: is learning technique and traditions from an experienced teacher high on your group's list of priorities? Do the majority of people in your Circle feel they are in need of structured instruction? What if involvement with another tradition precludes members' working with your Circle? Which group's scheduling takes precedence? By opening the discussion in advance, you may avoid the problems Copper Key faced. However, it may be part and parcel of Craft life that disagreement about the way things are done will rock a Coven from time to time.

Other conflicts arose when outside groups were not even involved. Moriah felt very strongly that spells should not be done by members of Copper Key; Ginger felt very strongly that spells were perfectly legitimate ways to exercise individual will on one's life.

"On one of our road trips, Ginger decided to do a spell to attract love. She followed directions from a book. Intent on bringing a lover into her life, instead of a specific person, she listed the qualities she most wanted her lover to have," Foxfire said. "Moriah stood to the side watching, obviously annoyed. Finally, she told Ginger she disapproved, but Ginger, who is, as her name indicates, a bit spicy at times, said that she believed in spells, that she would continue to do them, and that as Witches we could successfully execute positive spells. Moriah was clearly irritated by her response. That evening as Acacia and I led the Ostara ritual, there was an undercurrent of tension. Moriah was pulling away from the group."

Most other members fell somewhere in between the two. Mer-Nuit sums up how the Witches of Copper Key in general feel about spell-casting: "I consider when a spell is done properly, it is as though the Witch reaches out and touches the spinning Wheel of Fate. She may slow, speed, or stop the Wheel to get her desired results. And her personal wheel is like a gear in a universal set of gears, so that what she does potentially affects every other individual's wheel in the universe. As William Blake put it, 'To pluck the nearest flower/ troubles the farthest star.'"

The most important factor in any Coven is the trust between members. "You have to trust the individuals with whom you are Circling, not only because you need to work on personal issues, but because you can't really open yourself up to the energy in a Circle if you can't trust the people who are there," Laurel said. "Even if you aren't working on something private, it's a block. My teacher told me once that if you can't walk into a Circle and know why you're there, and be completely comfortable, without looking to the left and to the right, or before you and behind you, then you shouldn't be there."

If you are uncomfortable with any aspect of any work in which your Circle is involved or with what the Priestess for the evening initiates, you must be honest enough to tell the group how you feel, and allow them to explain. Hopefully their explanation will suffice and you will be able to participate in the activity. If you are still uncomfortable, it is better for you to excuse yourself from the meeting.

Eventually, Moriah became the first member of the Copper Key Circle to leave. She called a meeting at her home, inviting everyone to attend. "That night we discussed the direction of the group," Foxfire said. "We more or less voted to define ourselves as a practicing Coven, as we had been meeting for more than a year-and-a-day and a majority of the group felt they were called to walk a Wiccan path. Moriah felt more strongly drawn to Native American traditions. While she definitely believed in the power of magic, she did not want to explore it herself because she was afraid of unintentionally doing harm. Copper Key was ready to delve more deeply into the Craft, and Moriah chose to withdraw from the Circle."

Although the group was sad to lose one of the core who had been there since the beginning, the moment was bittersweet; Moriah's reluctance to self-identify as a Witch had prevented the group from taking Covenstead. Her decision to leave Copper Key benefited her. It also arose out of her concern for the other women; just because individuals do not walk the same path does not mean that either path is wrong or that friendships must be sacrificed. The method that Moriah chose to withdraw from the group was honorable. It also gave the group a chance to experience some closure in the formal relationship without forfeiting their individual relationships with her.

POSSIBLE PITFALLS

THE IDEAL Coven will be made of Maids, Mothers, and Crones with different backgrounds, interests, occupations, and even different orientations, heritages, and family upbringings. What happens when these varied people try to function in perfect love and perfect trust over an extended period?

"Once you are inside a Coven, you are really naked—there is no place to hide," Ginger said. "We can do an unbinding ceremony for someone, and of course we will know if that person really lets go. We can make a New Moon vow about our health, and everyone knows if we are putting forth an effort to make the changes we need to make. That close scrutiny is not something everyone is really comfortable with."

In the best possible situation, the differences in your members will serve to complement one another and you will be able to call upon those differences and strengths for the many roles that must be played to run a successful Coven. At times, however, you may find that the very qualities which you admire can become stumbling blocks.

"We went through the transition from an association to a community, and personalities did rub against each other, and those corners had to be rubbed off," Laurel said. "It's been true in every organization I've ever been in, from my business to church guilds to PTA."

In its first year, Copper Key spent a good deal of time worrying about how to make everyone happy and keep them coming back, fearing that any dispute would signal the end of the Circle. "This was really a group of peace-loving people, so they couldn't be confrontational even if it came to saving themselves," Laurel added. "Small groups would get together and talk, and say, so-and-so said this, or whatever, and nobody would confront the person."

But any group that wants to be a success must learn to deal with problems in a positive, proactive way rather than allowing the problems to create even bigger trouble. "I remember when we were planning our first retreat," Acacia said. "Briar had been meeting with Copper Key almost since it began. On her campus, she had been helping the Pagan Student Union get started. But when it came to her own relationships, she had not yet resolved the issue of coming 'out of the broom closet.' She was dating this guy from a fervent Christian denomination, and rather than telling him up front she was Wiccan, she claimed to be agnostic. This shouldn't have been a problem for us, but Briar decided that the best way to introduce the subject was to invite her boyfriend on the retreat. We all just let it go, hoping she would change her mind. On Thursday before we were leaving, she had still not told him just what it was that we planned to do for the weekend. My husband, who was on faculty at the college they both attended, was going with us. I told her on Thursday that she just couldn't bring him if he didn't know. She didn't agree; both of us spent hours on the phone talking to everyone else in the Circle and finally everybody agreed that she shouldn't bring him. We should have told her how we felt when she first brought it up, but no one wanted to be confrontational. I finally decided that the trouble it could cause my family and the group was more important than me being polite and passive."

Over the next few months, Briar became more and more involved with her boyfriend, but never shared her spiritual life with him. Finally, the delayed decision the group made the day before the retreat contributed to her decision to stop meeting with Copper Key.

A situation that was handled somewhat better occurred when they asked Ahriel to wait until she was of legal age to attend meetings of the Circle. While she herself was ready to jump into Coven life and to take an active part in it, she was only seventeen, and her mother was opposed to her involvement. When Copper Key learned of this, a decision had to be made: would they continue to participate in Ahriel's disobedience? Was Ahriel's freedom of religion the more important issue? One evening Ahriel admitted that she had lied to her mother about where she was going so that she could join the group for a meeting, and the women in the Circle resolved that a hard decision had to be made. It was agreed by all that Ahriel would not meet with the group until after her eighteenth birthday, if she was still interested in the Craft and in working with a Coven.

"If there is a problem, address it immediately," Laurel said. "We've talked about how some of us came from dysfunctional families, some of us were in dysfunctional marriages, or had gotten out of dysfunctional marriages, or some were in jobs where the work group was dysfunctional, and boy, does all that carry over."

After being together for a few months, the group began to understand some basic things about the way they worked together and the way it felt to be a Circle. In fact, one prospective new member came to Copper Key looking for a group that was raising cones of power at every meeting and "drawing down" regardless of who was in attendance. "At least we were savvy enough to realize that we didn't have any business doing that," Laurel said. The prospective new member was disappointed and returned to only one other meeting, but the group ethic was preserved and the individuals began to realize that to fully function as a Coven, they had to be careful about opening meetings to visitors.

More than one person who showed up for open meetings was not in a position to accept the responsibility of joining a Coven, because she had not yet dealt with other issues in her life. While some level of spiritual and psychic healing can occur in a group that is meeting to celebrate Wicca, anyone who has a substance addiction, is involved in abusive relationships, or has a psychological/chemical imbalance should be receiving the professional help she needs outside the Circle. "The Circle is not a psychotherapy group; it doesn't have personnel sufficiently competent to deal with those issues," Laurel said. "And even if it did, the Circle is not the place to deal with such problems." Individuals must be working toward positive goals in all areas of their lives before they are ready for the Coven experience, and before the Coven is ready for them.

Another difficulty may arise in a group where governance is a shared responsibility. When a strong personality is allowed to dominate decisions about the direction the Coven is going or to dominate individuals within the group it causes problems. If all members are moving toward the goal of becoming effective Priestesses, then all members should be given the opportunity to serve as Priestess without constrictive coaching from the sidelines. Members asking other members for advice is one thing; unsolicited directives and proclamations of "right" or "wrong" should not be part of a shared community. Your group may determine an outline of specific ritual aspects that each meeting should include; however, one person deciding the parameters of the ritual experience is more in line with a group governed by a High Priestess than by the whole. Address the problem within the context of the Circle when it first becomes apparent; don't let the "she said monster" run rampant, or you may find your Coven dissolving before your very eyes.

CONFLICT RESOLUTION

REGARDLESS OF the problems a group may face, the solutions always begin with the same ingredients: honesty, communication, and trust. Whether you are debating ritual technique, spell-casting, admitting new members, supporting public events, or addressing a personality conflict within the Coven, the same format can be used to get the group back on track.

Begin by finding a time and a place where all members can come together; stress the importance of every member making it to the meeting, regardless of other responsibilities—be certain they understand what's at stake. Perhaps your most diplomatic member should be put in charge of making the phone calls. Once the location and time are agreed upon by a simple majority, do not change either, under any circumstances. Moving meetings around and changing times leads to confusion and a sense of uncertainty, neither of which you want the group to associate with conflict resolution.

The location can be key to how the group interacts. For example, if there seem to be two obvious "camps" in the group lined up behind two strong individuals, do not choose either of those members' houses for the meeting. A restaurant may not be ideal, either, as members may not feel free to speak openly with other people around and waiters interrupting every few minutes to pour tea. The best location will be a neutral zone, like the bookstore where Copper Key first met, or a public park away from crowds, or the home of someone who is not caught up in the debate.

Once everyone has arrived, the first order of business will be to set up a ritual space. However, instead of following an elaborate script, the most basic elements should be used. Whoever is serving as

Priestess could simply offer her hand to the woman next to her, and say, "From hand to hand, the Circle is cast"; each person passes the phrase until all are holding hands. The Priestess could then offer a general invocation to the Quarters, asking for the inspiration of Air, the passion of Fire, the depth of Water, and the wisdom of Earth, followed by an invocation to the Goddess and God. However the Circle is established, all problems should be solved within its boundaries.

When everyone has settled into comfortable positions, the Priestess should introduce an object, such as a "talking stick" or a wand or a sistrum, which will be passed to the member who has the floor; a "no cross-talk" rule should be in effect. The Priestess will serve as a facilitator; she should remind the group that perfect love and perfect trust are the goals of all Circles, and that whatever needs to be said should be said. Should it turn into a personal attack on an individual, she must be ready to move the group back into constructive discussion. However, if someone in the group has been disruptive for one reason or another, she should be made aware that her behavior has caused a problem. If someone has not been showing up at Circles regularly, she should be asked why, and reminded of the responsibility of her membership in the group. The facilitator may set the meeting up perfectly, but if people are not willing to be open and honest with one another, nothing will be resolved.

If there are problems endemic to your group which cannot get resolved, at some point members will grow weary of having meetings to talk them out when nothing seems to be getting accomplished. At the first meeting on a particular problem, the group should give it a timeframe or deadline by which it is to be resolved: by the next Full Moon, or the next Sabbat, or the following New Year (Samhain), for instance. At the deadline, the Circle should reconvene on the particular issue, and if it still plagues the group, it may be time to consider a drastic step in the evolution of a Coven; it is called "hiving" by most Pagan organizations.

In this process, a person or a group of people from one Circle or Coven determines that the best way for them to practice the Craft is to leave the original group. At that point it is important to discuss the possibilities honestly, make a plan for a formal separation ritual, and determine that the two new groups will not bear grudges but will consider themselves an extended family. In fact, in most traditions, hived groups come back to meet with the Mother Coven on a particular Sabbat (Beltane is the most common).

"It's inevitable that people will leave: they grow, and they change, and they need to move on," Laurel said. "Their leaving, for whatever reason, needs to be kept as clean as possible. The Circle has that responsibility, and so does the individual."

If you and your group are to survive such a process, you must be ready to accept that change is a necessary and regular function of life; without death, there can be no birth. Paganism eagerly seeks out change and the cycles of living—you must be able to accept that part of the process if you choose to partake of the community and support that is Coven life.

JOURNAL ENTRIES

1. Ginger's experiences brought up these issues for me:

2. How comfortable am I in dealing with conflict? What role am I most comfortable playing during conflict resolution?

3. Confrontations among my friends make me feel:

4. These are elements I feel are necessary for a successful ritual:

5. How comfortable am I participating in rituals from someone else's tradition?

6. I think I could/could not serve as a facilitator for a group problem-solving session:

COPPER KEY RECOMMENDS:

Among Friends: Who We Like, Why We Like Them, & What We Do With Them, by Letty Cottin Pogrebin; New York: McGraw-Hill Book Company, © 1987.

Dreaming the Dark: Magic, Sex, and Politics, by Starhawk; Boston: Beacon Press, © 1982.

Getting to Yes, by Robert Fisher, William Ury, & Bruce Patton of the Harvard Negotiation Project; New York: Penguin Books, © 1991 (2nd ed.).

Hidden Agendas, by Dr. Marlin S. Potash; New York: Delacorte Press, © 1990.

8
FAMILIES
& COPPER KEY

HUSBANDS

SIX MEMBERS of Copper Key are married. Two husbands agreed to answer questions about how the Coven experience has affected their lives and their households, about their own spiritual beliefs, about parenting, and about loving a Witch. These two were chosen because of their very different attitudes towards Wicca and the Coven: Seal studies Wicca with his wife, and John remains a steadfast atheist; their opinions on everything from raising children to the time their spouses spend on the Coven are miles apart.

INTERVIEW WITH LAUREL'S HUSBAND SEAL

Author: How has your spouse's involvement with Copper Key and Wicca affected your life?

Seal: It has led to my becoming involved in Wicca. I have gone to Circles and festivals and I have been dedicated as a Grove student in a Wiccan tradition.

Author: What were your spiritual beliefs before you embraced Wicca?

Seal: I was brought up Methodist, and although I was kind of a prominent social Methodist, the religion didn't really take. At a fairly young age I was a scoffing agnostic/atheist, and I went through some internal conflicts. Having had hellfire and damnation pushed on me at an early age, it did take some time and effort to rid myself of all that. Then, through my twenties religion just wasn't anything that I particularly cared about one way or the other. It just didn't have any place in my life. In my thirties, Laurel and I met, and I joined the Episcopal church with her—she was already a member,—and I enjoyed it. I thought that it was a comforting faith-of-our-fathers sort of religion, and I enjoyed the ritual, but I certainly didn't buy into it to the extent I changed my belief system. I thought that the church was a myth much like other religions with a resurrected God. I had a little knowledge (of these) from reading The Golden Bough, but I had not read extensively. Oh, I was married once before, to a Roman Catholic, but that just didn't take at all. I went with her to mass only on Christmas and Easter.

Author: Were you married before Laurel began practicing Wicca?

Seal: Oh yes, we were both practicing Episcopalians. There's a joke about how you can leave the Episcopal church: you can either die or get religion. We just happened to have found the Pagan religion.

Author.:   Do you have children?

Seal: Yes, we do.

Author: How do you feel about them being exposed to the Craft?

Seal: I think it is a healthy thing, wholesome with a good belief system and positive values. I do worry somewhat about the children understanding the need for discretion. There is nothing they should be ashamed of, but basically Wicca is very misunderstood. They just don't have the ability to discern whom they can confide in and whom they can't. It's hard to expect young children to understand they must be discreet. I worry that if I tell them to be discreet that they might think Wicca is something to be ashamed of, but if I don't tell them to be discreet the news might get blabbed all over town and people will misunderstand.

Author.:   From your experience, what would you tell other parents who are considering practicing the Craft and who still have children living at home?

Seal: I really don't think I can advise them, because I'm uncertain about how it's going to turn out. Laurel and I made the decision not to involve our older children in the Craft at this point. Both are over ten years old and have been involved in the Episcopal Church all their lives. Our two youngest (under five) have been around during Circles and understand a little of what we do. They will probably grow up learning Craft values. It's been a hard decision to make, but I think it is the right one. I hesitate to give anybody advice, because I don't know whether the way that we're handling things is the right way or not. I think it is, but it's something I still worry about.

Author: You've met the women of Copper Key, and you've attended Circles and celebrations. What are some of your impressions of the Coven?

Seal: The women are very interesting, I enjoy their company. They can be a fun group, a lot of them have a good sense of humor. Though I probably know them better than perhaps any other spouse, I'm still on the outside. I'm not in the Coven, and my impressions are those of an outsider.

Author: How did you feel driving home from the first Circle you attended?

Seal: I can't really remember. I don't think it was anything startling or I think I would remember it better. I know I enjoyed the meeting. I had already seen Laurel do some solitary work, so I had some understanding of what would happen. I had also read some of her books beforehand. It was reassuring.

Author: What do you think is the most important thing Copper Key adds to Laurel's life?

Seal: Affirmation of the things that are very deeply feminine in her nature, her intuition, the way that she looks at things. I'm a left-brain sort of person, and she's a right-brain sort of person. We're both a bit off the norm in those directions. I think it gives her affirmation that the way she sees things is valid. Also, the women whom she has bonded with are a source of strength for her.

Author: Have you ever had moments of doubt about the Coven experience?

Seal: Well, we have a very committed marriage, we believe in cleaving only unto each other, so the whole undercurrent of sexuality that runs through Wicca bothered me a little bit. It made me feel uncomfortable, when, for example, in one altar setup, there is a scourge. I asked Laurel if that wasn't just a little weird, but she said that it hearkened back to medieval times. It was a technique for symbolic discipline and doesn't really have to hurt. I've always thought that just because the Catholic Church used scourges doesn't mean that the practice isn't strange. This is not to say that I've ever seen anybody in Wicca scourge, or even heard about anyone using it. As long as it's symbolic, I guess it's okay, but if it were really put to use I would find that troublesome.

Author: Have you had any doubts about her relationship with Copper Key?

Seal: No, not about Copper Key. When she worked with Hidden Grove, I found that a little more troubling. I never had any problem with Copper Key, even before I met them, because I understood from Laurel that it was a group of women who were trying to make some sense out of a religious tradition in a very non-threatening way. And I've felt good about everyone in the Coven I've met.

Author: What would you tell a husband whose spouse was about to start down this path?

Seal: Try to put aside your prejudices and look at it fairly, be open-minded. Don't be so rock-sure in your belief system that you think there can be no other valid way of thinking.

Author: Do you ever resent the time that Laurel spends with Copper Key?

Seal: Sure, sometimes. I think that any time you've got a really good marriage, and the person whom you're married to is the person you most want to spend time with, anything that takes your spouse away from you for any time you're going to resent. Laurel sometimes resents the time I spend on my job, but you have to learn to cope with those things, and you have to realize that you can't smother each other, even when you are really close. Some things just have to be endured.

INTERVIEW WITH ACACIA'S HUSBAND JOHN

Author: How has your spouse's involvement with Copper Key and Wicca affected your life?

John: It's made it much more complicated. Weekends socially are pretty much dead, seeing how New Moons and Full Moons and Sabbats and other wonderful holidays occur with much frequency, and preparations for those celebrations normally take up a good deal of her free time outside work.

Author: What is your spiritual background?

John: Well, let's see, it's diverse, I was exposed to many different paths from Southern Baptist to Catholicism to Nietzsche; I was an altar boy, I was a student of religions, I tried to read everything I could about all different paths, from Hinduism to polytheistic religions to completely monotheistic religions like Christianity, Judaism, and Islam.

Author: How would you describe your current spiritual beliefs?

John: One hundred percent, bona fide, dedicated atheist, which makes it difficult for my wife and I to relate occasionally. She loves people because she believes in a higher power, and the interconnectedness of all people. She has an immense well of love for human life and people and is compassionate and empathetic when she sees suffering. It comes out of her belief in the interconnectedness of all life and the big wheel and all that kind of stuff. It shapes her compassion to a great degree. And I have a tremendous love for all people and I want them to live good lives because once they're dead, there ain't nothing else.

Author: Were you married before or after your mate found Wicca?

John: We were married before she found Wicca.

Author: Do you have children?

John: No.

Author: If you do have children, how do you feel about them being brought up in the Craft?

John: I wouldn't want my children brought up with any set of beliefs. I would like them to be educated to think for themselves and investigate many different belief systems, including Christianity.

Author: How would you feel about them being exposed to the Craft and Craft ideas?

John: Exposure is fine. Forced participation would be quite different. Mandating their attendance at a Circle, for instance, I think would be inappropriate.

Author: Have you attended a Copper Key Circle?

John: Yes.

Author: How did you feel driving home after that first meeting?

John: The first meeting was an Ostara ritual, the first that I was exposed to. They were getting together on the banks of a river and throwing something in. I thought that it was quite bizarre that nine or ten well-dressed individuals were sitting around a painted egg meditating on it before throwing it into the water.

Author: What do you think is the most important thing that Copper Key adds to your spouse's life?

John: Strength. It gives her strength to voice her own opinions, it gives her a grounding.

Author: Have you had moments of doubt about the Coven experience?

John: Moments, no. Prolonged periods of regret, yes.

Author: Regret? Could you address that?

John: I was very supportive of my wife pursuing her spirituality and I tried to be very helpful in trying to find information for her and seeking out authorities. I have regretted doing that.

Author: Why?

John: Because the people that I was able to put her in touch with I believe were phonies, and perhaps dangerous.

Author: Was that Copper Key?

John: No, another group.

Author: So how do you feel about Copper Key?

John: Um, as far as my wife's relationship with Copper Key, I occasionally resent the amount of time she dedicates to this group. The relationships are still very new but incredibly intense, almost like a summer camp experience... I've purposely distanced myself from the group but know all the women in the group, even spent time socially with about half of them, and I respect most of them for their intelligence and their integrity and their power, but on the other hand I am concerned that sometimes they are investing (particularly my wife) too much of themselves into a group consciousness. And when something that doesn't exist corporeally, like a group, like Copper Key, starts dictating daily routines and necessities and priorities over, say, spouses and children and earthly responsibilities, it concerns me a great deal.

Author: Are there particular events that stand out for you as examples of this?

John: Planning, interruption of previously scheduled things. The precedence of the Moons and the Sabbats and other meetings over everything else.

Author: Can you name a specific example?

John: My wife went to one of the rituals in another state, and came damn close to catching pneumonia because she wanted to stay outside in the rain for a part of a ritual. On another trip, out of the city environs, perhaps considerations like the owners' property and the risk they were taking weren't adequately addressed. I worry about their safety, probably a little bit more than they do.

Author: Safety physically or emotionally?

John: Both, primarily physically, they are mostly all strong individuals emotionally. And together, they're a formidable bunch. But proclamations of "I'm a Witch" in the city in which we live is not wise. In the United States, and in Western civilization in general, to separate yourself out and say "We're Witches" might make you part of a larger community, I'm not sure how large, depending on what sources you read...but Western civilization doesn't recognize that as a subgroup or as a protected belief system.

Author: What would you tell other husbands whose mates are about to start down this path?

John: Well, Wicca is a very life-affirming spiritual path. The teachers of Wicca and the students of Wicca in and of themselves are fine. They expand your vision. Like all powerful ideas, Wicca makes you think about things differently, and that's very helpful. I would advise someone whose spouse is about to get involved to sit down with her and discuss what that's going to mean beforehand. She should not suddenly have this extended relationship with a bunch of strangers. When your spouse becomes very close to a group of people who have a religious experience every other week, they suddenly become part of your life indirectly, whether you want them to or not. Kind of like being born into a family that you didn't ask for, but suddenly you've got aunts and uncles and the like. You don't necessarily have to like them, and they won't necessarily like you. Unfortunately, unlike a marriage where you both go into it with a full knowledge of faults and good points, you don't get that with a group. If your spouse decides to join a Coven or be a founding member of a Coven, you can be supportive and say, "That's great, I'm glad you found a path, and I'm glad you found a group of women or men or a community in which to worship," but it becomes a pain in the ass real quick. I don't think that the amount of energy my wife puts into her Coven is a subtraction of the amount of energy she gives to me, it's not that they benefit at my expense or vice versa, but sometimes it feels that way, particularly since I'm not a follower of Wicca or a believer of Wicca or desirous of further studies.

I do read all my wife's books, most of the time before she does. I feel competent to discuss Wicca, its tenets, its belief system and its tradition. As a pseudo-scholar of history, I was very concerned with the false statements in some of the literature that weren't based on history or on research of artifacts, or of ancient languages. Some of it seems to me to be a modern creation from about 1920 onward. There are other trends in Wicca that I've read that I am very impressed with, that take in most of the pre-Christian era of Western Europe, but often they fail. But there's nothing wrong with creating new myths.

Author: Is there anything about Copper Key you'd like to add?

John: I'm amazed it worked. I know that you are doing this book as kind of a guideline, to help other people in other cities, but I'm not sure that what Copper Key has accomplished is replicable, because the impetus for Copper Key's success was the work of primarily five women, in my opinion. I think the strength of the individuals, my wife being one, the strength of their personalities, the fact that they are very organized and thorough, dotting all their "i's" and crossing all their "t's," is what made Copper Key possible. I think it's wonderful, even though it is a pain in the ass sometimes and I sometimes resent the organization for the amount of time my wife puts into it, and I resent the Coven for the relationship that it's had with my wife, because it's on a level that I apparently haven't achieved.

Author: That's a pretty strong statement.

John: I think it's like when one spouse resents the parents of the other, or the siblings of the other, because they know the spouse differently, not necessarily better, but they have a different angle.

Author: So do you see the Coven as being a family that your spouse has joined?

John: No, not really, in my definition of family...I think my wife has joined a community, a tight-knit community with a shifting hierarchy, or an amorphous hierarchy, but a community, a community that cares about each other. They go out on the limb for each other, they're always there for each other for physical and emotional support, but I don't think they themselves know where they draw the lines. I think a lot of them are at risk, not knowing where Copper Key stops and their professional lives begin, or where Copper Key stops and their family lives begin, and that worries me, because they're all parts of other communities, too, not just Copper Key. Even different religious communities, different professions, different families, and I'm afraid that sometime soon the boundary is going to smash into something or someone who didn't want to be aware of Copper Key, and that that could get messy and drag everybody into it. Once a member was going through a custody battle and I was afraid that my wife's picture would end up on the front page of the paper and she would be identified as a Witch. In our city that could mean harassing phone calls or a fire bombing or loss of employment, loss of profession, business, things like insurance, all sorts of things. I'm a firm believer in everybody's right to believe in whatever they want to believe, "I'll fight to the death for your right to say something I don't agree with." But I personally didn't want my wife going through it or even me, I don't think it's worth it.

The first time the group was out of town together was in a rural area where a Witch might just disappear and nobody would ask too many questions. So that worries me. And it's not just the publicity, it's also that their relationships with their families, with their co-workers and friends are important, as well. I don't think groups like Copper Key are safe or healthy for all concerned until a member can go down to her local Coven's ritual space, just like you can go to a tabernacle of the Latter Day Saints, Mormons, or Seventh Day Adventists, or Catholics, or Buddhists, or a Muslim mosque, or whatever; I think there needs to be a Wicca ritual space where a Coven can gather. There needs to be some sort of respectability given to it or I believe that there are going to be more difficult times ahead for the members of Copper Key, and I would hate to see those women get hurt because they're all fantastic.

DAUGHTERS

THE COPPER Key Coven includes seven mothers. The children range in age from newborn to twenty-something. Two of the daughters agreed to talk about their experiences since Mom became a Witch. "Tasha" is twelve years old, and recently began going to a public school after being home-schooled for several years. "Jade" is twenty-nine and attends art college. Both have met the women of Copper Key.

INTERVIEW WITH MER NUIT'S DAUGHTER TASHA

Author: How old were you when your Mom first told you she was going to follow this spiritual path?

Tasha: She didn't exactly come out and tell me. I guess I was about nine or ten years old. She was meeting with these friends of hers, the Cakes for the Queen of Heaven, a women's spirituality group. I knew most of the people. We went on a little camping trip and had fun, we went on a couple of picnics and all, and I didn't really mind. I teased her about the Witch stuff, I called her a "broom jockey," I think I got that off the television show *Bewitched*. After a while, she got involved with two new groups. One was Copper Key, and I didn't really know much about that, and the other was Hidden Grove, I didn't like that too much. She joked about the tattoo she would have to get to be initiated, and I thought that was gross.

Author: So how do you feel when you go to these meetings with your Mother?

Tasha: I don't usually go to the meetings, I usually try to stay about as far away as possible. Sometimes it's kind of fun, you know, candles, and things like that, rocks, and herbs and things, but most of it I don't like, like all the ceremony stuff. Most of the time I just go into the back room, I don't normally get involved.

Author: Do you know some of the other children of the Witches of Copper Key?

Tasha: Yes, I know Laurel's kids and Orchid's daughter.

Author: When you're all together do you feel uncomfortable or is it more like you all have something in common?

Tasha: Well, yeah, it's all right, we're friends. We just go upstairs or somewhere else and have fun, sometimes we spy on the grown ups.

Author: How do you feel with the kids at school?

Tasha: Well, I don't tell the other kids about it, 'cause, well, you know, people get teased enough for belonging to a mainstream religion, so I keep my mouth shut.

Author: How do you feel about spiritual issues for yourself?

Tasha: I don't know, I'm just thinking about it, going along and learning. I mean, I know the things that I would not join under any circumstances, like fundamentalist types, cults, the "Waco Wackos".[1]

Author: Have you been learning about the Craft from your Mom?

Tasha: I just watch it. I like the nature things, learning about old holiday ceremonies. I don't think I'll be in Wicca or Witchcraft when I grow up.

Author: Have you seen anything different around the house since your Mom has been involved?

Tasha: An altar, but it's not set up all the time. But we have a key hanging over the door, and some special candles around the house. Lots of books. She has different jewelry now than before. She was going around wearing a naked

---

[1] David Koresh and the Branch Davidian cult of Waco, Texas, involved in an armed siege with the FBI in early 1993; nearly 100 people, including children, died in the fire that ended the siege.

pendant[2] which I thought was kind of sick so I made her stop. I don't know where it is now.

Author: Do you do anything different around the house now from what you did before?

Tasha: Nothing really.

Author: Have you read any of your Mom's books?

Tasha: Some of the interesting historical type of things, but not many of them. In fourth grade I ran into a little bit of trouble with some kids at school, so I thought I would make some get-rid-of-your-enemy spells, that type of thing. It didn't work.

Author: Did you ask your Mom about it or is it something you did on your own?

Tasha: I asked her, and she said that anything I do will come back three times, so I shouldn't be doing anything negative. I just wanted to get the kids off my back.

Author: Has that been your only experiment with magic?

Tasha: I've done a few little things. I've made a couple of Voodoo dolls, but I was kind of doing that kind of thing before, because I have a friend at school who makes Voodoo dolls out of Kleenex. She was playing with them at lunch on Monday. We kid her about it. I don't know what her religion is, but she doesn't have Wicca in her family.

Author: So is that interesting to you?

Tasha: Well, yeah, I have friends who have lots of different religions. Most of them feel the same way about them that I do. Parents all have different religions but we all feel that we should decide for ourselves.

---

[2] Venus of Willendorf figure.

Author: If you knew a girl your age whose mother had told her she was going to become a Witch, what type of advice would you give her?

Tasha: Well, don't get all upset. Don't say, "I'm going to go shave my head," or "I'm never going to speak to you again," or anything like that. Yes, it's really going to drastically affect your life, but it's not really different than joining any other religion.

Author: What about when you grow up and have kids? What if one of your daughters or sons wants to look into Wicca?

Tasha: That'd be all right with me. I'm not going to force any religion of mine on my kids. If they start getting off the edge, like if they went from doing Wicca and found people into Satanism or something, I would say, "Hold it. You shouldn't be doing that sort of thing." But I don't really mind about Wicca. Some of the things in Hidden Grove were a little bit weird. As long as things didn't get too weird I wouldn't mind.

Author: When your Mom first got into Wicca, I know that she was very concerned that you be comfortable. If you could go back to the first week you knew about Copper Key, how did you feel?

Tasha: I have a few entries in my diary about Mom going to meet with Witches, but I don't really remember much about it. I was really kept separate from it. I didn't know what Copper Key was, I mean, it was never an earth-shattering new thing. She just sort of progressed from a Cakes group to Copper Key to Hidden Grove and now to a CUUPS chapter,[3] so I've never been totally involved in it.

Author: Have you gone to any of the CUUPS meetings with your Mom or any of the Cakes or Goddess rituals at the church?

---

[3] Covenant of Unitarian Universalist Pagans.

Tasha: No.

Author: How do you think things are now with your Mom? I know Hidden Grove is not her focus now, how do you feel about that?

Tasha: One thing I didn't like about Hidden Grove was some of the men in it. I heard her talk about one of them who was always coming on to the teenage girls. I thought that some of the things were weird that way. And she griped about it a lot too, she didn't like the rigid ceremony so much either. I don't miss that group at all. I'm happier that she is back working mostly with Copper Key.

Author: You'll be in eighth grade next year. Have you had classes on religions of the world or anything like that yet?

Tasha: In Sunday school at the Unitarian Church I learned about Hinduism, Islam, Shintoism, and things like that. I also went to Catholic school for one year and made my First Communion when I was six. So that's the only study I've had.

Author: In school when somebody talks about Witches, around Halloween time, or when you talk about the history of Witches in this country, do you have to bite your tongue to stop from telling them about the Witches you know?

Tasha: I don't think anybody's mentioned it. The only religious issues that do come up are things in the papers like the cults, the abortion issue, and gays in the military. The media call those religious issues. The only problem that I've had is when I went to a 4-H camp. A girl with very religious parents wasn't allowed to go to a party. I wanted to say that it was kind of stupid having those kinds of rules, but my Mom had warned me not to say stuff, because most of the girls are probably from backgrounds that wouldn't like it too much, so I just don't say anything.

Author: Do you think that being a Witch and being in a group like Copper Key is good for your Mom?

Tasha: Well, she's got friends, and she seems to be happy with it. It's not harmful as far as I can see. They're not doing peyote or anything. It's good as long as she's not getting hurt or hurting anybody else.

Author: What about the time she spends away from you and your Dad?

Tasha: Lately I've started getting ticked off at her because last week she went out for four nights and then on Saturday we went to an Isis lecture. She went away for half the day on Sunday. On the weekends I don't like her going out. Usually it's for CUUPS and church. I'm just like, "Hey, it's the weekend and I want to have some fun," and she's spending all the time with her friends and there's no time for me.

Author: Is she normally away that much?

Tasha: Lots of times. Like when she was in both Copper Key and Hidden Grove, that was totally clogging up the schedule. But then I was in home school so I could see her during the day and I could stay up late to see her when she came home, so it wasn't that much of a deal. But now I've got an eight-hour school day and a set bedtime, so I have only about seven hours a day to see her, and when she's gone three or four it's not much fun.

Author: What do you think a good compromise would be, say if somebody who reads your interview has the same problem?

Tasha: Don't get into too many things at once. She's president of CUUPS—she's involved in planning the big festivals, and she's in Copper Key—I hardly ever get to see her.

INTERVIEW WITH GINGER'S DAUGHTER JADE

Author: To your knowledge, how long has your Mother been in the Craft?

Jade: Oh, I don't know, maybe four years. I remember her being involved in that Cakes class at the Unitarian church. Before that, we probably talked about it because I had done some reading, like the books by Starhawk, and had had some interest in the Craft myself. I am a Lesbian and have been involved and out for almost ten years. I heard about the Goddess and was reading books by Starhawk long before my mother had even expressed an interest in it. I know I have gone out with women who are involved in Moon Lodge; it is a very accepted religion in my community. Maybe that helps make it not so kooky to me, because I respect it as a religion. I wonder if there is no respect in the community at large, because the Craft is not mainstream and people just don't hear about it.

Author: What do you think has been the biggest change in your Mother's life since she entered the Craft?

Jade: I think at the time she started doing it she was going through a lot of changes. She'd gone through a lot of .therapy, dealing with her memories and her own personal happiness, and to me the Craft and therapy are connected with an overall positive change. She's happier, more fulfilled. I think it's given her a really strong sense of community and a circle of friends who make her happy.

Author: Do you ever resent the time your Mother spends on her Circle?

Jade: No, not at all. I'm real glad. I mean, I'm an adult, we don't live together, we make dates and see each other a couple of times a week, and that's fine. I think that people who have a religion that makes them feel fulfilled and happy are more interesting. To me, the time we spend together is even better because she's a happier person, she's got more stuff going on.

Author: Have you met the women of Copper Key?

Jade: Yes, some of them. I've not been to any ceremonies, but I've been with them at social functions. I've even brought friends of mine to holiday gatherings, and everybody seemed to get along great.

Author: You mentioned earlier that you had some interest in Wicca before. Is it your current spiritual path?

Jade: Well, maybe the set of beliefs are similar to mine. I'm not a person who goes in for group religious activities. I find it interesting, but any kind of organized religious activity is just not real appealing to me. I know that if I had to pick a religion, this is the one I would be in, but still, it's not my thing. I have a circle of very close friends whom I talk with about spiritual and personal issues, but I can't imagine discussing my personal feelings in a group of strangers. It's a little too "touchy-feely" a practice for my tastes. It's great, but it doesn't suit me.

Author: Are there aspects about it which you do like?

Jade: There are not a rigid set of rules and laws in the Craft by which to live. There is room for a person to make moral choices on their own, and to live and grow and learn from experience, versus the typical Judeo-Christian value system. I like that Deity has both male and female aspects, because the idea that the Supreme Being is only one gender is completely ridiculous. What makes up the Supreme Being for me would be all the energies that make up life.

Author: What was it like spiritually when you were growing up?

Jade: We were not a really religious family. When I was little, and my mother was a middle-class housewife, I remember being taken to the Methodist church, which was very milk toast. I don't know what children who grow up in charismatic or energetic religious groups feel like. I didn't think about spirituality really one way or another. After my parents got divorced, Mom was on this quest for happiness or whatever, and she went through a lot of things, sometimes self-help, or feminism, or Eastern philosophy. She went through a hippy born-again phase. I remember going to a total immersion baptism at the hippy church. So I guess no matter who's right, she's covered. I felt at the time I was in my own little world. I was a real moody kid. What she was doing I never thought of as spirituality. She was trying to find her own happiness, and these were the ways she was looking for it. I was more affected by the fact that she was not a happy person than by any group that she belonged to.

Author: What advice would you give to someone else whose mother was about to head down the Wiccan path?

Jade: I think that for a lot of people, especially my age or younger, there's a lot more openness and interest in Wicca. Of course, it depends on your background; I'm sure there are people from very conservative religious backgrounds who might have trouble with it. I guess I would tell them to keep an open mind about it. I think it's also important to realize that it's hard for teenagers and young adults to understand that parents may have needs that are outside of their relationship with their children. I think a lot of times it's hard to view parents as human beings. Considering the parent as a person might help.

Author: Is there anything else you'd like readers to know about you, your mom, or your situation?

Jade: You can't be afraid of letting your mother grow and change. The happier she is, and the more she learns and is fulfilled, the better the relationship will be. And that goes for all relationships, whether parent-child, or friend, or lover. You have to let them grow.

ON PARENTING
& THE CRAFT

BEING A Witch and being a mother are not two diametrically opposed occupations; in fact, the women of Copper Key feel very strongly that their children should be exposed to the life-affirming beliefs that they share with one another.

"I really feel like my parents cheated me," Laurel said. "I should have started studying Wicca as my daughter has, at her mother's knee. I should have been sweeping a Circle at three as she did and going to informal Esbats with my mother or my grandmother or someone in my family. I should have been raised knowing the stuff that I've had to learn on my own, so that it would have become second nature to me. You should just absorb spirituality as you grow up. I thought for a long time that fate had dealt me a low blow, that I had been catapulted into the Priestess role without ever having had a chance to be the Handmaiden to an experienced Priestess."

Copper Key welcomed children at some of the open Circles that were held during their first year-and-a-day together. Yule is a natural occasion to invite them in, and Copper Key even had Laurel's youngest daughter sweep the Circle. She practiced for hours and hours before, and was happy to be going to one of her mother's meetings. However, children's attention spans being what they are, Acacia's husband John volunteered to sit in the family room with holiday videos playing on the television, waiting for the inevitable: three of the children ended up spending most of the evening with him.

Before deciding to include children in your celebrations, it is important to consider the feelings of the entire Circle; particularly on occasions when concentration and meditation are of extreme importance, your group may not wish to include anyone too young to sit quietly for an extended period of time. Like the decision on whether or not to include men in your rituals, the decision to include children should be made by the group as a whole.

Occasionally the group must take into consideration that not every mother has the resources to hire a babysitter for the group's meetings. You may wish to work out a system where the teenaged children or husbands or significant others provide childcare wherever the Circle is meeting, or offer to meet at the home of the woman who needs to keep an eye on her kids. Should there be no other solution, your group should do the best it can with young ones weaving in and out of the ritual space. The only caveat is that much of what is said on occasions like Samhain is of an extremely personal, sensitive nature; use your best judgment in determining when to include whole families.

Problems for mothers with young children in the Craft are compounded when they are dealing with a spouse who doesn't support their religious life. Orchid's husband refused to learn about her spiritual choices and in turn disapproved of her taking their daughter to informal gatherings of the Coven. She talked about the problem with Copper Key during one of their retreats:

Ginger: What is his objection to raising her in the Craft?

Orchid: He feels that I'm putting her too far out of the mainstream, and it will be hard for her to fit in with her friends. The holidays are different; he's afraid she'll be ostracized. You know how badly you want to fit in when you're a teenager.

Mer-Nuit: I think that's true. If her friends' parents know you are a Witch, they're not going to let their kids come to your house.

Orchid: But Maroona has me as a mother. I'm a Witch, I'm a Pagan, that's my religion, that's how I feel. That's just an accident of her birth. I think it's real sad that there are kids born as Jehovah's Witnesses that are not allowed to celebrate holidays with the rest of the society. What about kids brought up as Jews? What happens to them in school?

River: Kids in high school never feel like they fit in anyway, and the ones who do hit their peak at seventeen and the rest of their lives is downhill. There are worse things.

Orchid: Also, the female empowering element of Wicca, I think it is very important for Maroona. Already at eight years old she's upset because she thinks she's fat, she's asked me why men like thin, blond, blue-eyed, big-tittied women. And she's eight years old.

Ginger: She's a gorgeous petite child with brown hair.

River: When I met Maroona, I thought she was a very bright, articulate child who seemed very interested in what was going on. I'm afraid if you tell her, no, you can't come, then she might wonder, "Why? What's wrong with it?" or worse, "What's wrong with me?"

Orchid: Exactly. I can't hide it. I've never been false or fake with her and I'm not going to start now.

Ginger: There is the question about whether to give children religion at all.

Orchid: My husband thinks we shouldn't give her any religious direction. I think that's wrong. I think there's a void there and somebody's going to fill it. I want her to be exposed to the Unitarian Church and to the Pagan ideals which I can instill in her. If she decides to go off and become a fundamentalist Christian later, that's her decision.

Ginger: I think the tolerance inherent in Paganism is really an amazing thing. Sabina's older daughter is in a state of rebellion. She's joined the Catholic church, and she made an issue of it with Sabina; she came over and said, "I've joined the Church," then stood there and waited. In return, Sabina said, "Well, it's not something that I would do, but I hope it's the choice you like." Her daughter just stood there, amazed.

River: I think that's because Christians have a monotheistic form of belief, and we are polytheistic—we've got options. There are many different ways of things being sacred, and that lends us the ability to think about things diverse rather than narrow. The Hindus have much the same philosophy. I might be very much into a certain Deity, and you might be more closely tied to some other God or Goddess, but we can come together and worship. We can recognize the divine in both our ways of thinking, and it is not a problem.

Ginger: None of us is out to convince the other that one way is wrong. We do share a similar world view, and in that broad spectrum all is acceptable.

Orchid: And you learn that acceptance in a small group like this, and that acceptance radiates out into so many other areas of your life. You become more accepting of people in all your relations.

Ginger: The first time that you teach or learn hate or intolerance, it's like a straw or a siphon that pulls everything down. We have to be careful not to say, well, the Baptists are wrong, because then a child has the idea in his mind that if the Baptists are wrong, then the Jews could be wrong. And this kind of thinking leads to things like, well, if they're wrong, then maybe that race is wrong, then maybe that gender is wrong, then maybe I am wrong. It's eventually self-defeating. You can't liberate with one hand and persecute with the other.

Author: So how do you keep children in the Craft from inheriting the ideas of the society?

Orchid: Tolerance is inherent in the Craft.

River: But there are so many places we have to be careful not to let intolerance in, whether we are discriminating against some other tradition of Paganism or some other faith altogether.

Ginger: We have to be careful, too, about our language and the symbolism, and the ideas we put forth. For example, we call the Goddess into the Circle using a name and a persona, Demeter, Hecate, Inanna. Then we refer to our Mother Goddess the Earth. I'd think a child might be a little confused. I think the idea of universal sacredness is the most important tenet of our faith—if everything is sacred, then that man over there or that race on the other side of town or those people in that synagogue are sacred and there is no room for hate.

Orchid: None of which is bad for a child to be exposed to.

River: Will your husband read your books, will he read the book about us?

Orchid: No. He refuses to. I think he thinks this is a phase, and he can wait me out.

Foxfire: I think men fear the strong female element.

River: Even if he thinks it's stupid, it's part of your life, and he should acknowledge and respect it for being part of your life, regardless of his personal feelings. I started getting into feminism and Paganism at about the same time I was dating a guy who was an atheist. His exact words to me were, "I don't know why you're wasting your time on this being willfully ignorant." I didn't push it on him, but I stood my ground. Eventually he picked up a book or two, decided it wasn't so bad.

Orchid: Well, I've quit trying to tell him about it—I just wait for him to ask me questions and he does sometimes. But he doesn't want to attend *any* ceremonies. I've invited him, but he won't meet with the group. He keeps saying, "This is silly, it doesn't mean anything, this magic junk, spell spell spell, what a bunch of shit." You know that Persephone's apron we made at Ostara? I've been sleeping with it under my pillow every night and on the Full Moon I'm going to bury it or do something with the shell. Empowering my wish for luck this year. He hadn't noticed it under the pillow, until the other night when he reached over to me, put his hand under the pillow and pulled it out. It's tied up in a handkerchief, with dried flowers and string and stuff. He said "Is this what I think it is?" I told him, "It's just a little spell." "In my bed?!?! I can't believe it. I have a right to know what goes on in my bed. I don't want magic in this bed." All of a sudden, it's real.

River: That boyfriend I was talking about, whenever we made love he made me take the pentacle off, because he was subconsciously afraid that a bolt of lightning was going to come down on him if I had a religious symbol on. I don't know what he was afraid of, but he didn't even like to kiss me when I had it on.

Orchid: There's some deep-seated, primal fear men have of us, I don't know what it is.

River: But in pre-Christian times, men worshiped the feminine. The men who worshiped at the temple of Ishtar were basically giving themselves up to female power. Men went through the Elysian mysteries and that was basic primal female power. They respected it.

Orchid: So do you think it's just a result of being ingrained by the Patriarchy?

River: If it's ingrained, then feminism is doomed.

Ginger: I think it's that women are so tied in to the life-death-rebirth cycle that men cannot be associated with—we give birth—

River: And we bleed without dying—

Ginger: So underneath it all, regardless of Christianity or the Patriarchy, women force men to recognize and accept death, even when they don't want to. Christianity even goes so far as to say that women don't make babies, God makes babies out of the ribs of men. They said Nature is a lie, you will not fall and die. Men in their hearts know that they will die, and women are here to remind them.

River: But you can't say that men aren't connected to death — look at the men who go into war and make death.

Ginger: The death they're connected to is the end. The death women are connected to is the beginning of life. Men aren't connected to death in a cyclic fashion. Men may choose to make death, but women are thrown into that by the very nature of our bodies. The one thing Freud was right about is that biology is destiny. He took a wrong turn after that, but he was right about that one point.

River: I think you're right—I think Judeo-Christian traditions deny that part of us and Paganism embraces it.

Ginger: That's why there are so many more women in the Craft than men.

River: Plus it's also easier to see the oppressor when you're one of the oppressed. The dude on the horse has no opinion on the horse, but the horse has a definite opinion about him. Think about the Hindus who worshiped Kali in her most awesome form—eating the intestines of her con-sort—they think that you cannot worship the Goddess until you can appreciate her as your own terror and devourer. Sure, I think there is an inherent fear of death and the unknown in everyone, but I think Paganism works through that to acceptance, where patriarchal religions deny it and actually feed off it to keep people in line.

Ginger: Annie Dillard talks about this one type of insect that kills frogs by injecting them with a poison that dissolves them and then it literally sucks the frog dry. So what you find is this empty frog sack. I think the reason her book sang to me is that it is truly Pagan—to be Pagan, you must be able to accept the horror of that frog's death if you also love the flowers in the spring.

River: If you don't have death, you don't have life.

Orchid: Exactly.

Acacia: And women are constantly forced to remember what they are—men are not.

Ginger: I can buy all the suits, be a workaholic, anything you want, but every twenty-eight days something is going to remind me that I belong to the earth.

Acacia: And men will never feel the quickening of a new life — they can never have that sense that another life is inside of them.

River: I've got this theory that Freud was way off on penis envy— it is a case of classic transference. It's pregnancy envy— guys cannot get pregnant. They are jealous of it, so the whole thing is sour grapes.

Acacia: They can much more easily deny nature, because they don't have that part of life in them.

Foxfire: Not only are we reminded every twenty-eight days, but even when you reach my age and menstruation stops, you are forced again to deal with the cycle of life. Men may have a psychological menopause, but we have to deal with it both emotionally and physically.

River: Men actually do have a hormonal cycle. I think I've read that it's like 24 days or 32 days. If we and they would pay attention, men have got the same emotional PMS that we do.

Ginger: Before I had my hysterectomy, my friend Laura came to live with me. Laura had been through the Change. She hadn't had a period in eight months. She lived with me for three months and started having her period again.

Orchid: Because you were still bleeding?

Ginger: Yes.

Foxfire: I was with a woman who was in her early fifties, and I was in my late thirties. When we moved in together, she started having periods. She was like, "Where did this come from???"

Orchid: I've never lived with another woman so I didn't know about this. What effect would that have on someone who was going through menopause and who might also have teenage daughters who were bleeding?

Ginger: I tell you what I think it would do if we were living intergenerationally. I think that it would moderate the menopause phase.

River: I think you're exactly right.

Ginger: Your body would get a chance to adjust to its own hormones levels—maybe we wouldn't need to take all the estrogen pills they dose out. I think if you were living with a group of women and young girls starting their periods, all those pheromones, we'd all be a lot healthier naturally. You know how it's physically triggered? Smell.

Orchid: Really?

Ginger: Yes. It's pheromonal, triggered through air.

River: We were talking about some of the menstrual rituals where you paint yourself with your menstrual blood. But you don't need that much—just a tiny dab of the blood under your nose and it stops your cramps. There's a physiological basis behind that.

Foxfire: When my daughter moved out, I stopped having periods.

Ginger: That would make a natural cycle.

River: You know what you were saying about intergenerational living, what was the normal way to handle periods in aboriginal European societies? The menstrual hut. And the women ended up being out there all together. Those on their periods, the young women who were just about to come into their cycles were the attendants who brought food and rubbed backs, and the older women would go out there and teach.

Ginger: The older ones were definitely not excluded, and there was a practical reason for this.

River: There's an old saying: "The Craft is nothing but practical."

While they may not have solved Orchid's dilemma, at least she had a place to voice her concerns. As Seal, Laurel's husband, said in his interview: "I don't know how it's going to turn out. Our two youngest children have been around during Circles and understand a little of what we do. They will probably grow up learning Craft values. It's been a hard decision to make, but I think it is the right one. I hesitate to give anybody advice, because I won't be able to say whether the way that we're handling things is the right way or not. I think it is, but it's something I still worry about . . ."

If you are a parent dealing with issues of rearing children in the Craft, you may want to look into some of the positive literature available for children about Witches, or subscribe to newsletters for children of Pagans. Networking with other Pagan parents is never a bad idea—look for articles and advertisements for parents in your favorite newsletters. If you feel that your children need a broader religious base, consider attending your local Unitarian Universalist Church. They offer world religion courses for children and teens, and host activities such as camping trips, community service projects, and "lock-ins" for their youth groups.

Whatever religious heritage you provide for your children, remember that they have their own path to walk in this life. You may provide a positive role model and important moral values for them, but how they eventually choose to worship and celebrate their experience of Deity is up to them.

JOURNAL ENTRIES

1. If my significant other decided to join a Coven, this is how I might feel:

2. I think my own significant other feels this way about my involvement in the Craft:

3. If I were a parent, how would I deal with the Craft and my children? Would I share this faith with them? Would I expose them to many different religious beliefs?

4. Picking any single relationship in my life to reflect upon, this is how my own involvement in the Craft affects them, and also how their religious beliefs affect me:

5. These are my responses to each of the four interviews in this chapter:

COPPER KEY RECOMMENDS:

The Family Wicca Book, by Ashleen O'Gaea; St. Paul, Minnesota: Llewellyn Publications, ©1993.

The New Golden Bough, by Sir James Frazier; New York: Criterion Books, ©1959.

Children's Books:

Elidor and the Golden Ball, by Georgess McHargue; New York: Dodd, Mead, & Company, ©1973.

Strega Nona, by Tomie de Paola; New York: Simon & Schuster, ©1975.

Strega Nona's Magic Lessons, by Tomie de Paola; San Diego: Harcourt Brace Jovanovich, Publishers, ©1982.

9
FREEDOM
OF RELIGION

TARA'S STORY

Tara agreed to help a university instructor and police officer, present the Wiccan faith to a group of law enforcement officials and social workers during a two-day seminar on alternative religions. For the attendees at the conference, the goal was to broaden their personal awareness of cultural differences and to help them understand that alternative religions are valid and protected by the Constitution, and that their jobs include protecting everyone's freedom of religion. Their questions and her answers follow her preliminary introduction which detailed how she came to the Craft and why.

Hello. My name is Tara, and I am a Witch. I got into the Craft through a long process full of frustration.

I started out the way most nice girls do, in a nice Christian family. I was raised Methodist and when I became older I became an Episcopalian. I was and am very strongly a feminist. At that point in my life the term Feminist Christian was an oxymoron. The Christian religion is patriarchal and hierarchal. When you start out saying, "I believe in God the Father Almighty," when 99% of your priests are male, when the Bible says, "And God created man in His own image," when even the churches that do not believe in interpreting the Bible literally still interpret the myth of Adam and Eve so that it's all the woman's fault, then for me there was something very wrong. But I listened and I studied and I tried very, very hard to work within the church.

In my particular church I was the first female Senior Warden, which is kind of like the Chairman of the Board, and oddly enough, I got more hassle from the women of the church than the men, because women were not supposed to be leaders. Men make policy and women make coffee. Well, I don't make very good coffee, but I make pretty good policy. And I got more and more frustrated, resentful, and angry, and I kept thinking: women are half the world, and in the churches we're not given a chance to speak. Our needs are not being addressed, especially in the Episcopal Church, which is closely tied to the Roman Catholic church, which is *very* anti-women. I couldn't take it any longer. I was trying to go to Church and I was trying to be a good girl and fulfill all my mother's expectations and wishes and be there with her on Sundays, but it finally got to the point where I could not in good faith stand up in that church on Sunday mornings and say, "I believe in God the Father Almighty, maker of Heaven and Earth, and in Jesus Christ His only son, our Lord," because I didn't and I don't.

I believe very strongly in a supreme being. I don't believe that supreme being is male or female. I believe that supreme being is both. And neither. But in my practice at this point in my life, I like the image of the Goddess, I like worshiping a female deity who is the Mother, who is nurturing, and caring, and loving, and not judgmental, and who says, "You're okay exactly the way you are." And for me the Christian church didn't do that, it said you're okay if you don't practice birth control, and you're okay if you never ever ever think about having an abortion, and you're okay if you do as you were told, and you're okay if you don't question that God created man in his own image and that women were an afterthought. And for me that wasn't okay any longer. So I did what I usually do when I'm confronted with a dilemma: I started reading everything I could get my hands on, the first being, *Stranger in a Strange Land*, by Heinlein. In this science fiction, Michael is an Earth-being raised by strangers on Mars, and he comes back to Earth with this idea that "Thou Art God." You are God and I am God and all of us are a part of God. That made a tremendous impact on me, because it didn't say I am worshipping God, it said I am God and I am Goddess, and so are you, and so are you.

Later on, about four years ago, I got hold of a book by a woman named Merlin Stone. She collects myths, and she's sort of an anthropologist. She wrote a book called, *When God was a Woman*. She had done her research and gone on archaeological digs. She talked about the ancient, ancient times, before there were patriarchal religions, before, when people were hunters and gatherers, before we all knew that the men in this room had an impact on where babies came from, everybody worshiped the Great Mother. She was the symbol of fertility, because She was the only evidence of where life came from. Women gave birth. They still do. Therefore, the Mother gave birth to the world. And every ancient culture, every one of them, worshiped a great Goddess. Whether she was Isis, or Astarte, or Innanna, or Yemaya, or Spider Woman, every culture worshiped a great Goddess. She's called the Woman of a Thousand Names and of No Names, because we don't know all the names. I hadn't known that, so I read all the stories of all the great Goddesses. Some of them were fun, and some of them were fascinating. I read all the old myths and I wondered, "Why have we lost this balance between the female energy and the male energy? Why is everything male-dominated?"

I decided I wanted to find a religion and a belief system where my identity as a woman is validated, as important as yours is as a man. And I want something that is inclusive and is participatory. I think the thing that drove me craziest of all when I went to church is that I couldn't talk back. That man in that black robe could stand up there and interpret the Bible or preach a sermon, and say anything he wanted to, but I couldn't talk back because I was supposed to sit there in my little pew in my little dress and be quiet. Well, that's not my nature. I had some valid questions and I had some points that I wanted to discuss, except that there's no avenue for that. But in Witchcraft, we do everything in Circle. We are a group of equals. There will be a Priestess or Priest who is running the Circle that night, who is officiating, but that rotates. When I am Priestess, I am not going to stand here and you're not going to sit at my feet in nice little rows. We are going to sit in an encompassing circle, and it is participatory. Everybody has a part in it, everybody does things, everybody is involved. You're not sitting there listening to me tell you the Gospel according to Tara. Now I could do that all day long, I'm more than happy to tell you the Gospel according to Tara, but that's not what the Craft is all about. What I believe is that Thou Art God, and I am Goddess, and my beliefs and my opinions are just as valid and just as real as that man's who is standing up there on Sunday morning. He may or may not have been more educated than I am or educated differently from me, but my opinions are just as good as his.

So I started reading, and continued reading, *When God Was a Woman*, and I read *Goddess of a Thousand Names*, and I read a book called *The Spiral Dance*, by a Witch named Starhawk, from California. Hers was a how-to book, telling you how to cast a Circle, how to gather herbs, etc. I read everything I could get my hands on, and I thought, "I like this. This feels right for me."

One of the things I liked best about it was that there are laws. Wiccans do not believe in the duality of God and Satan; they do not believe in a supreme good versus a supreme evil. We do believe in the duality of God and Goddess, and the balance of male and female energies. But we also have a very strong system of ethics. It's not full of "Thou shalt nots," it's not based on guilt and it's not based on payment of your sins by eternal suffering and damnation. It's based on a set of laws.

The first one is, "Harming none, do what you will." As long as I am not harming anyone, what I want to do is okay, and what I feel is okay, and what I believe is okay.

The second law is kind of fun—the law of threefold return. What I send out to you, I'm going to get back, threefold. If I send out hate, hostility, and evil, if I send out resentment, I'm going to get all that back. If I send out love and acceptance, if I stop in traffic and let somebody in ahead of me, I'm going to get that back threefold. That's one of the basic beliefs. And that manifests in some of the funniest, little bitty ways that you don't even notice until you stop to think about it. I'll give you an example: the other day, my sister was having a really, really rough time. Things were not going well at work, and her youngest son, who's fifteen, was having a case of the teenage-itis, and everything was driving her berserk. I brought her flowers. Just a handful of carnations and some of those purple spiky things and I put them in a bud vase on her desk. No real reason, I just did it to help her feel better. A few days later, I was sitting at my desk and somebody sent me a giant bouquet of flowers to say thank you for a project I had done. What I had done for her came back to me threefold. Coincidence? Maybe, but I don't think so. What you send forth, you get back. If I send to you hatred, if I hate you and I can't stand you and I think you are abominable and the slime of the earth, I'm going to get those feelings back. Somebody's going to feel that way about me.

And the third law is, what you do has consequence in this world. Which means I'm responsible for my actions. The three kind of tie together. It's not a law that will let you say, "I'm not responsible for anything and I can play perpetual victim, and it's not my fault." Well, I did it, and it is my fault, and I will bear the responsibility for it. So it all ties together. For me that was comfortable because I believe in being responsible for your own actions. I don't like some of the things in our culture that have helped it become a culture of victimization. I don't like my youngest nephew being able to worry his mother, and everybody saying that that's okay—he's just a teenager. Well, no, he's responsible for those actions and he's responsible for that harm that he's causing. So these beliefs drew me to the Craft. And we also believe that each of us creates our own reality. I am creating my tomorrows. For those of us who believe in reincarnation, I'm creating my next lifetime, right now, right this minute, by what I do. To me that makes sense, and I like things that make sense.

So I started looking around and I started thinking, "Is there anybody out there who feels this way too?" When you start on this kind of path, that's your first experience. You think there's nobody else but you who thinks this way, and you don't know where to go or what to do, and you feel very isolated. I went into a bookstore, and asked the owner if there were any other women like me out there, because it's not only a bookstore but also a gathering place for women and their friends. Remember, at this time I was still going to the Episcopal church and I was still sitting in that pew and I was still fighting those battles. She said that there was a group who were going to get together there at the store in a couple of weeks. She gave me a phone number, and I called.

I told the person who answered the phone who I was and what I was doing and she said, "Yes. We'd love for you to come." So I went, and there were seven women there that first night. We did a small ritual, and we talked about ourselves, who we were and where we were coming from, and what we were doing, and did we want to continue with this, and we were completely terrified. We were not terrified of each other, we were terrified of society as a whole. I don't want my house firebombed, I don't want to take on the Fundamentalist Christians, although I would because I believe in my first amendment right to say and to believe what I want, but I don't want to have to do that. We were scared. But this was important enough that we decided, "Okay. Next Full Moon let's try to do this again." And all of us absolutely did not know what we were doing.

We all started on basically the same level. There were only a couple of us who had been to other Circles before and had at least seen how it was done, but it felt right and we felt like we were at home. And I've been there ever since.

Traditionally, a Coven has up to thirteen members, and that's for a couple of reasons. Number one is that small groups are much more manageable than large groups. In any kind of large group you don't get to know each other as well. Right now I think we are at ten. We've had various people drop out, and somebody moved away. People do this for a while and then decide that this is not *their* answer, so they move on; that's to be expected. So that's where we are and that's how I got here.

WHAT THE LAW WANTED TO KNOW ABOUT WITCHES & COPPER KEY

After Tara's introductory remarks, the police officer opened the floor for questions. Keep in mind that the audience consisted of roughly forty people—some thirty-odd policemen, one policewoman, and a small group of social workers. Here's what they asked Tara and how she responded:

Audience: You said that you were grappling with some issues and that led you to look into this way of life. Did that just come up because of your education, your religion, or because you saw something in the Craft that led you where you are now?

Tara: Probably it was my reading and my education.

Audience: Since you got involved with the Craft, have you thought about going back to the Episcopal Church since they are allowing women priests now?

Tara: They are beginning to accept women in the clergy, that's true. My current church affiliation is Unitarian Universalist, and my minister is a woman. Even though the Episcopal Church now accepts women as clergy, they still believe solely in a male god and still refuse to use gender-inclusive language. Next Sunday when you go to church, I want every one of you to try something for me. I don't care what religion you are, unless you are Wiccan; when you go to church and you listen to the Bible and you listen to your preacher preach, every time he says the words "man, father, or son," in your mind, switch it to "woman, mother, or daughter" and count the number of times you do it. I guarantee that you'll be surprised. And I know many people say that using the word "man" is meant to encompass everyone, but language is a very powerful thing, and it doesn't do that. I think we need the balance. I don't worship solely the Goddess, but at this time in my life I identify with her more strongly. I also worship very strongly the male principle.

Audience: I'm curious about the racial composition of your Circle.

Tara: The Circle with which I practice is 100% European-American. There are other Circles that I know of that are a little more balanced racially.

Audience: I noticed that when you said "Isis" you pointed to your earrings, and that you talked about different Goddesses. Do you have some special closeness to Isis? When you say, "We worship the Goddess," which one are you talking about?

Tara: We worship the Goddess in all kinds of different forms. When each of us serves as Priestess, we normally each have an affinity for a different Goddess form. I do worship the Goddess, but I also recognize Her different faces. In fact, it often depends on what issue I want to address. When I am worried about my friend who has HIV, I will probably address the Oriental Goddess Kwan-Yin, who is the Goddess of compassion and mercy. If my love life is screwed up, which is fairly frequently, I might talk to Astarte, the Goddess of love. I am only speaking from my experience, I'm not talking for the Coven, but I think that there is one Goddess and we speak to her many aspects when we speak to a particular name.

Audience: How many Covens do you think are in this area?

Tara: I know of three; I am sure there are more that I don't know about.

Audience: Do you have much association with other types of groups like Satanists? Are you ever in contact with individuals of those groups or have you ever met anyone from them?

Tara: We haven't yet. In fact, the Women's Spirituality Forum we participated in was probably the first public thing we've ever done, and there was no one there that fits that description.

Audience: You seem comfortable talking to us about it, but how do other people react to you? Do you tell them at work that you're a Witch? Do you find acceptance?

Tara: Actually, I work with my family, so I am somewhat freer with it than if I worked somewhere else. My mother thinks it's a phase I'm going through, like when I was a little girl the only candy I wanted to eat was chocolate covered raisins, but I got over it. She thinks I will get over this too, and that I will come back to the Episcopal Church. I have my doubts. The Unitarian church is very aware that they have Pagans and Witches in the church. We have a CUUPS chapter at the church, which is the Covenant of Unitarian Universalist Pagans, and there are several of us at that church who belong to the group. They prefer that we use the word "Pagan" rather than "Witch," simply because of the connotations of the word, and I have no problem with that. In many ways it's easier, because I don't have to immediately fight the stigma that I ride a broom and turn people into frogs. But I am semi-open about it in most areas of my life.

Audience: Are most Covens from the Unitarian denomination?

Tara: No, the Covens I know of and the individuals I know are from all different backgrounds. We've got one woman who is still a practicing Episcopalian. Most of us now belong to the Unitarian Church simply because they accept us. I have a friend who is Wiccan and who belongs to a Congregational church. We don't want to be totally separate, we want to be a part of the community in which we live, and we want you to accept us for who we are.

Audience: Could you define the term "Witch" for me?

Tara: There are so many definitions. I like this one: "A Witch is a person who will stand up and say, 'I am a Witch,' three times." It's someone who believes in the duality of Deity, in both the God and the Goddess, and someone who believes in the laws I was talking about earlier, and who does not believe that there is a single God who created the heaven and the Earth. And Witches do not believe in Satan, the devil, or even the concept of that kind of evil. You or I may commit acts which are considered evil or negative or dangerous, but as far as the concept that Satan causes those acts, we don't believe that.

Audience: Your major holidays are different, correct? Do you celebrate Christmas, do you do the tree and that whole deal?

Another Audience Member responds: The tree was theirs first.

Tara: That's true. We celebrate Yule, which is December 21st, the Winter Solstice. The tree was ours first, and the idea of the child being born on that day is also ours. One of the oldest myths is that of the Goddess bearing a child at that time, the young Sun King. And then he goes through changes over the Wheel of the Year, in which we celebrate eight holidays which mark the progression of the Goddess and the God until the Sun King is reborn again at Yule. Christianity borrowed our date.

Audience: Do you exchange gifts on that day?

Tara: Yes.

Audience: Could you tell us the holidays?

Tara: Sure. The first is Yule. The next one, like many of them, has several names. It is called Imbolc or Brigid, and is February 2nd. It celebrates the young God growing. The third is Ostara, Spring Equinox, and it celebrates the young God and also the young Goddess, who also goes through a cycle of growth. They are celebrating and playing and enjoying the Spring. The next, Beltane or May Day, is still practiced in parts of England with the Maypole; it celebrates courtship, love, and sex. Summer Solstice is celebrated next, it is the marriage of the God and Goddess, and it starts his journey to the underworld. Lammas is August the first, which is the celebration of the first harvest, and then we celebrate Mabon, which is the Fall Equinox, and the final fruits of the harvest. Samhain is next, which the Christian world calls Halloween. That is the time when the veil between the worlds is the lightest, when communicating with the dead is supposed to be the easiest. For us it is a time of death and rebirth in many aspects of life, where you take stock in your life. And then is Yule, and the cycle starts all over again. Our Ostara corresponds with the Christian Easter, and there are other holidays which have correspondences in modern religions.

Audience: So the birth and death and resurrection of Christ doesn't mean a thing to you?

Tara: No. We believe in birth and death and rebirth, but we don't believe in that kind of resurrection. And we believe in willing sacrifice, but not in that kind of martyrdom.

Audience: Is this why a lot of women go into this?

Tara: I don't know. I do know that many people who follow the path have a need for balance and a need for a religion that is participatory. We are a constantly evolving tradition, and each one of our Priestesses brings a very different sort of energy to our group and will perform a very different kind of ritual for them, whereas, particularly in many Christian churches, the ceremony is always the same. Of course, there is a beauty in that also, and a part of me misses that grandeur sometimes, but the balance is not there for me.

Audience: Does your religion allow or disallow you to be a member of or participate in government or civil affairs?

Tara: We can do anything we want to do, as long as we harm no one. If I ever wanted to run for office, say the State Legislature or anything else, I don't think that if the public knew I was a Witch that I would get elected. And it wouldn't be because of who I am or what I have to offer, but because in this time and this place it wouldn't happen. I'd be wasting my time and a whole lot of energy.

Audience: How long have you been practicing the Craft?

Tara: I've been working with a Coven about two years.

Audience: What do you think is the usual age for a Witch?

Tara: Our group ranges from about 22 to 50, so we have a pretty wide range. I know of another group that has only college-age members. There's another, which is totally Dianic, and their age range is probably the same as ours, though they are a much bigger group. It just depends.

Audience: I've seen the word "Gaia" in print—what is that?

Tara: Gaia is the original Mother Goddess. In scientific terms, it is the theory that the Earth is a living organism.

Audience: Who determines who gets into your group? How would they go about it?

Tara: First, say if you were interested in the group, you would come to two New Moon ceremonies, and then you would be invited to a Full Moon ceremony. After that, the members of the whole group would sit down and talk about how we felt, whether or not you fit in. Then a couple of us would meet with you, to see how you felt, what we had to offer you and what you had to offer us. Then, you would attend a Sabbat ceremony, and you would go through a learning period with a specific one of us to help you along over a year-and-a-day period.

Audience: Have you ever had anyone in your group and about halfway through the group decided that she was not really who they needed?

Tara: No, but there have been people who about halfway through have decided that Wicca was not the path for them.

Audience: What are some of the books that your Coven uses to train new members?

Tara: We use Starhawk's book, *The Spiral Dance* and *The Women's Spirituality Book* by Diane Stein. We use many different myths, including some of those included in the new book, *Women Who Run With the Wolves*. There are so many different books. Many of the book-stores around carry them, and others that they normally classify as "occult," which means hidden rather than general knowledge. What we use depends on which one of us is doing the teaching.

Audience: I think I've always thought that witches had to be born into families to be a Witch, but I think what you're saying is that you can learn to be one.

Tara: There are those of us who are born with a gift. I heard a woman speak a few weeks ago who was born knowing certain things, things she had no business knowing particularly about people, and when she was young and in school it was very disconcerting. Her mother finally told her, "Look, you are a Witch, I am a Witch, and it goes no further than this house, because it will get you and me in trouble." So there are those of us born with things like that, but the rest of us feel drawn to it and feel drawn to study it. We feel that we are born to find the path, it has just taken us a while to get there.

Audience: Do you who have families, do you try to get your children into it and into practicing Witchcraft?

Tara: We try and teach our children our rules and our ways. Right now the Circle is all women, and so the women with young girl children occasionally bring them to the celebrations. But we firmly believe that everyone has their own path to follow, so when the children are old enough, whatever they choose as their own religion is fine.

Audience: There won't be any conflict if they try to go into some other denomination?

Tara: No.

Audience: Do you know of anybody in law enforcement who practices the Craft?

Tara: I don't know of anybody, but that doesn't mean that there aren't.

Audience: When you all come out publicly do you hear any rumblings from the "Anointed Soldiers of God?"

Tara: Not yet, and I would just as soon not.

Audience: Do you practice magic?

Tara: Yes.

Audience: How do you know that when you do as you will you're not harming another?

Tara: That's the catch. It sounds real easy, but it is very difficult. You have to be very conscientious about all your actions. I can do something, thinking it is the most benign thing in the world, but if the consequences are that it harms someone else, then I have done the wrong thing. I have to be very careful.

Audience: Do you have any connections to Covens around the country?

Tara: There are Pagan Gatherings all over the country, including this part of the world, and there is quite a bit of networking that goes on. There are national organizations and national publications which keep us all in touch.

Audience: On TV, you see a lot now about Save the Earth and the environment. Is there a connection between this and Witchcraft?

Tara: Witches very strongly believe that we are all connected, and that we are all one, and that it is our responsibility to be a part of the movement that is saving the Earth because that is our home and we are connected to it. The Bible teaches that God created the Heavens and the Earth and that man was given dominion over the heavens, the Earth, the animals, and the fish of the sea. Witches don't believe that; rather, we believe that we are part of the interconnected web of life, and whatever happens to it happens to us. For example, I'll use the spotted owl because it is such a popular issue right now. If the spotted owl goes extinct, in some way that is going to diminish each one of us. In our group, several are married, some are single, one is a Lesbian. If she experiences prejudice because of her sexual orientation, then all of us are harmed, because we are connected. If you experience prejudice because you are Black, then all of us are harmed. If the rain forest is depleted because we are greedy, then all of us are harmed.

Audience: Do you ever go Skyclad, and if so, what determines when you do and when you don't?

Tara:	We have not yet. We are getting ready to, I think, though primarily weather determines it. If it's cold, I am not going Skyclad. We are very practical people. If it's twenty below I am not going to let part of me freeze off. Being Skyclad is a very positive experience because it removes a lot of negative body image experiences. As women, we are taught that we are supposed to be a size eight and that we are not to take up very much space. When you are in a Circle, and you see women and men of all different shapes and sizes, you really see the beauty in each person, and you realize that to be yourself means you don't have to meet someone else's expectation of your body.
Audience:	How do you go about finding mates in your religion?
Tara:	It really depends. Some of us were married before. There's not really a way to find a mate.
Audience:	Are the spouses supportive?
Tara:	Again, it depends. One of our Sisters' husbands is very, very supportive; one of them is an atheist so he thinks it's all a waste of time anyway; one is agnostic; one has felt very threatened by the whole thing, but is beginning to come around, and now understands that we're not going to turn him into a toad. If we ever open the Circle up to both men and women, I don't think he'd be one of the ones to join.
Audience:	Who made the popular image of the Witch as a woman in black riding around on a broom, with a crooked nose and warts, and why?
Tara:	The Catholic Church. It started even before the Inquisition, but that really did it.
Audience:	Who knows what a Witch is supposed to look like?
Tara:	Well, I'm a Witch. I look just like you do.

Audience: Do you think maybe making it an ugly image made it easier to burn them?

Tara: Certainly. It started out more as a political movement than anything else. Some people wanted to get rid of the women and widows who owned property, and this was also the time when men were beginning to take over the practice of medicine from the women healers. Different sources say from 100,000 all the way up to nine million people in Europe were killed as Witches, and 80% of them were women. It was very much a woman's holocaust.

Audience: What was the determination of whether or not they were Witches?

Tara: All they had to do was offend someone. All you had to do was have a child blame her measles on a woman, and she would be taken in for questioning. They were tortured until they named another twelve people who were part of their Coven, whether those people actually were Witches or not. I read recently that those people who have family traditions that have survived those times say that more than 90% of the people that were killed were not actually practicing the Craft.

Audience: What type neighborhood do you live in, and do they know you are a Witch?

Tara: Most of them know that every so often there are women that come to my house and we draw the drapes. Some of my neighbors, who are also my friends, do know.

Audience: Well, if I knew a Witch lived in my neighborhood and I was mad at someone, I might come to you to work me up something.

Tara: Except that I wouldn't do that, because it would be harming another person.

Audience: How would you feel about one of us coming to visit your group, just to sit through a meeting and see what it's like?

Tara: I would have to go back and talk with the other women, maybe not even my own group but some others that I know; it might be possible. Some groups do have open meetings occasionally. Leave me a list of people that would be interested. Some of the people that I know in the Craft are very afraid of going public, because they've got a lot to lose.

Audience: You say that according to your beliefs you would not harm anyone, but do you or anyone in your Coven feel you have the power to manipulate nature, like turning people into frogs, for your own personal gain?

Tara: I don't feel that I have that power because I choose not to have it. We use the phrase "turning people into frogs" as more of a play on the old stereotypes than anything else. If I were going to seek to do that, I do have a list of people I think I would experiment on, and for some of them it would be a step up on the evolutionary ladder. But while I am not interested in pursuing that type of power, I think that the power does exist to manipulate nature in every religion. If you want to use your individual power negatively, you don't have to be a Witch—look at Jim Jones. I can't imagine anyone I know who is following the Wiccan path who would ever do anything even as remotely destructive as he did, and he claimed to be Christian.

Audience: How do you feel about being called a feminist? I am hearing mostly the woman's point of view today, and the male seems to be secondary.

Tara: Everything I'm saying today is coming solely from my own point of view, and it might have been more fair to you to get someone who works with a gender-balanced Coven. Witchcraft celebrates both the God and the Goddess, we celebrate the energy of both. It is not the stereotype of women being passive and nurturing, and men being active and aggressive, but we do believe that there is a difference in the energy, and we celebrate them as the Goddess and the God. In fact, one of the ancient images is of the Horned God, and that is probably where the image of Satan came from, except that the horns that the Horned God wears are the two crescents of the Moon, an ancient female symbol. He represents fertility and the harvest. We believe that that energy is there, and that we need both of them. I believe that one of the reasons our society is in such trouble is because I am not the only person negated by living in a patriarchal society, but so are you men, because you're not allowed to realize a whole part of your identity either.

Audience: When you look at the Branch Davidians do you think that it is just the government persecuting someone for their religious beliefs or do you think that the government is getting rid of a dangerous element?

Tara: In that particular case, I see a little of both sides of the issue. I don't think that anything that calls itself a church needs to have an arsenal of weapons. I think the Bureau of Alcohol, Tobacco, and Firearms had some valid reasons for going in there. While I don't know all the details, I think that there may have been a feeling that "these people don't fit in with the mainstream, let's do something about it." At this point, from everything I've read, I think that the people involved on both sides will all be in need of some help.

Audience: You've made it sound like all the Witches in the world are Glenda the Good Witch from the Wizard of Oz. Are there Witches or people who claim to be that cross over and break the rules?

Tara: Well, certainly, unfortunately there will be. There are some that claim to be teachers who use that power to convince people to do things that they are not comfortable with. If I tell you I am the only way that you can ever be initiated as a Witch, and the first thing you have to do is sleep with me or give me $500, and you really want to be a part of it, you might just do it. I wish I could say that it didn't happen in the Craft, but the sad thing is that it happens everywhere. It happens in offices, in Catholic churches, it happened in that Branch Davidian situation. I would love to be able to tell you that all of us are Glenda the White Witch, but we are all people first and foremost. Power corrupts, and absolute power corrupts absolutely. If I say I am High Priestess, and you don't know much about what you're getting into, it will take you a while to feel comfortable enough to tell me that I'm full of garbage if I'm abusing that power.

Audience: You've made reference to the Catholic Church. Is there more tension between what you believe in the Craft and the Catholic Church than any other religion?

Tara: No, I'm sorry if I have made it seem that way. I refer to it more often because it is the oldest Christian church, and the history between the two goes back the furthest. They were involved in stamping out the Old Religions that were matriarchal. Honestly, I probably fear the head of the Southern Baptist Convention more than I do the new bishop of the diocese.

Audience: Do you think the Catholic Church has made a lot of changes since Vatican II? Is it more to your liking since then?

Tara: I agree that it has made a lot of changes, but I don't know that it will ever get to my liking, because any time a man who is celibate stands up and tells thirty Bosnian women that have been raped over and over and over again that it is their duty to bear those children, it will never be to my liking. I think it is unrealistic for a priesthood that is all male and supposedly all celibate to tell women how to live their lives. That's my biggest quarrel with the Catholic Church as an institution.

Audience:	You said you believed in magic. Have you performed any, and what was the outcome, or if you have not performed any, have you seen it done?
Tara:	I've done a little bit on my own. The outcome has been positive, but I am very cautious about it, as I have been studying magic only about four years total. I think it is a very powerful force. One of the definitions of magic is the ability to change things at will. I want to be very, very sure of my sense of groundedness and my motives before I mess with anything that powerful.
Audience:	Have you seen other people who have gotten into it more?
Tara:	Not in person, no, but I have heard about and read about people who have gotten into it more. As I said, our Coven as a whole is relatively young.
Audience:	Do women get into the Craft basically because they're jealous of men?
Tara:	I don't think jealousy is the right word. I think women get into the Craft because they may be drawn to the opportunity for equality. It is fun and wonderful to be Priestess, it is also good for the ego, but I don't think that jealousy makes it feel so right.
Audience:	What would happen if someone in your group did something against your beliefs? Who would discipline them or would you just cast them out?
Tara:	We don't discipline each other because we believe that we are each responsible for our own actions. If one of the members of our Coven did something that we all felt was very, very, very wrong, then the Coven would sit down and talk about it as a whole, and explain why we thought it was wrong, and if it could not be resolved and the majority of the group felt too uncomfortable to work with that individual any longer, we would probably ask her to leave. We've never had to face that, so it is hard

for me to tell you theoretically what we would do, but that is generally the way we solve most problems, by sitting down calmly and discussing them.

Moderator: At this time, we've been here for over an hour, why don't we take an extended break, and let anyone who hasn't wanted to ask a question in front of the crowd ask her questions one on one.

Following the lengthy private Q & A session, Tara added:

Mostly, they all want either to come with me to a Circle, or to have me come talk to their churches. One guy wants me to come talk to his Officer's Training Classes on a regular basis. Most wanted to know if there was a group in their area, and if they could get in contact with the groups for information. I couldn't answer them, really, because over the three states represented here today, I don't know of any network that they could plug into for information. Many wanted to drive back here again to come and watch a Circle and see what it is like to be involved in the ritual. I'm going to ask around, maybe someone will be willing to let them come.

One man asked me that if I believed in the powers of magic and in developing those powers, if at some point we would no longer need doctors because we would be able to heal ourselves. I told him I didn't know, and that most of the healing we have done is on a psychic level rather than a physical level, but that I would like to believe that at some point that will happen.

I tried very hard to make eye contact with everybody in the room, because I wanted for them to see me as a real person rather than some symbol or some weird aberration.

One of the women asked me again about marriage, and if I wanted to get married would it have to be to a man who was Wiccan. I answered that if I fall in love and want to get married, he wouldn't have to be Wiccan, but he would have to be accepting of me for who I am, and if he were not accepting of me and thought that in the relationship he could change me, he'd be wasting a whole lot of time.

THE FIRST
AMENDMENT & YOU

SINCE DECEMBER 15th, 1791, the United States has operated under the following constitutional amendment: "Congress shall make no law respecting an establishment of religion, or prohibiting the free exercise thereof; or abridging the freedom of speech, or of the press; or the right of the people peaceably to assemble, and to petition the Government for a redress of grievances." Technically, Wiccans are free to practice their religion; in fact, Supreme Court rulings regarding religious freedom tend to protect the individual from encroachment by the government *whether the religion is organized or personal.*[1]

However, public opinion and social pressure to conform to supposed societal norms often impact the lives of people practicing alternative spirituality or trying to make independent choices about their personal freedom. In a public forum in 1992, presidential candidate and "Religious Right" spokesman Pat Robertson said the Equal Rights Amendment would "prompt wives to leave their husbands, kill their children, practice Witchcraft, destroy capitalism, and become Lesbians."[2] His attitude faces all women, not just those in the Craft, who exercise the rights granted them under the Constitution. Women in any of the categories above—divorcees, Pro-Choice advocates, Witches, proponents of government taking care of the people, and non-male identified women—are at an even greater risk of losing their individual personal freedoms to a community and a nation that is not ready to deal with their diversity.

---

[1] "Moving the Line Between Church & State," by Elena Neuman, THE WASHINGTON TIMES, May 18, 1992
[2] The Associated Press, Oct. 10, 1992, dateline: Des Moines, Iowa.

At a Pagan gathering held in 1991, one of the seminar topics was how to handle custody disputes when the "W" word is involved. A group of close to forty women attended the seminar; about a third of them had been personally involved in such disputes. One woman had not seen her children in over two years because a judge had ruled that a "self-proclaimed Witch" was not fit to rear children. While every case is more complicated than just one issue, the question remains: If she had not practiced an alternative spirituality, would the court have decided that she *was* fit to rear her own children? How much did the popular stereotypes of Witchcraft affect the judge in the case? While no one in Copper Key has had to fight this particular battle, every mother in the group has been concerned at one time or another about the possibility.

"Of all the Pagans I know, River and my friend Yodwin are the only two who are completely open about it," Mer-Nuit said. "And Yodwin has lost more than one job because of it." The Civil Rights Amendment of 1991 does cover rights of religious freedom in employment issues, although a test case for Wiccan rights has not been heard at this writing.

Intolerant communities also bring pressures to bear which force conformity to societal norms. Case in point: A store called "The Magick Moon" in Jonesboro, Arkansas, was forced to shut down after being open less than a month because church leaders in the small town convinced the owners' landlord to evict them.[3] The store specialized in Wiccan books, jewelry, ritual equipment, and the like. Landlord Steve Griffin even arrived to deliver the eviction notice "flanked by two ministers from the Wood Springs Church of the Nazarene."[4] Legally, Griffin was within his rights, as a month-to-month lease was in force. However, his words, "If you left tomorrow, it wouldn't be soon enough,"[5] certainly give one an insight into the impetus behind his decision. Ethically, most Pagans believe that the landlord's actions were equivalent to the complicity of Protestants when the Nazis came for the Jews—and over one hundred Pagans

---

[3] INSIDE EDITION, Sept. 16, 1993.
[4] "Do You Believe in Magic? Witching Hour: 'Fort God' vs. Born-Again Pagans," by Laura Shapiro & Daniel Glick, NEWSWEEK, Aug. 23, 1993.
[5] Ibid.

linked arms with supporters and marched in that town on August 1st, 1993, where a crowd of 3,000 looked on, jeered, or joined in the protest.

Copper Key was well represented at the march. Mer-Nuit, River, Foxfire, Tara, and Willow (a recent addition to the Coven) all made the long-distance drive to support the store owners. "The evening before the march, my father-in-law said very seriously, 'Be careful tomorrow,'" Mer-Nuit said. "He has never talked about my religion, and I was very surprised he would even pay attention. It made an impression on me, that he really seemed to think I was putting myself in danger. And he flew helicopters in Viet Nam."

Coverage of the event included the Cable News Network (CNN), the Associated Press, and others. Eighty local police officers, sheriff's deputies, and state troopers kept the event peaceful,[6] although the Pagan group did run into a band of Christians who hurled insults and arguments at the peaceful marchers; the Pagans answered by singing, "We Shall Overcome."[7]

"Going to the march I was really scared," Mer-Nuit added. "It brought back all the stories the nuns used to tell us about early Christians being fed to the lions . . . but this was, ironically, Pagans being fed to the Christians." The owners of The Magick Moon are still looking for a place to reopen their store; so far, thirty-two prospective landlords have turned them down.[8]

Why is it that Christians who supposedly "love their neighbor," feel the need to force minority religions underground? "A local Baptist church advertised that they were going to show an educational film, entitled 'Devil Worship,'" Mer-Nuit said. "I attended the showing. The movie included the statement that Wiccans were Satanists and that the Horned God was really Satan. It insinuated that Wiccans are low-level Satanists who will find out the real truth about the 'cult' we are in when we get initiated to higher levels. It stated that Wicca was

---

[6] "No Praise as Witches, Christians, Raise Voices," by Larry Young, THE ARKANSAS DEMOCRAT/ GAZETTE, Aug. 2, 1993.
[7] "Magick Moon's Quest for Freedom," CIRCLE NETWORK NEWS, Vol. 15, No.3, Fall, 1993.
[8] Shapiro & Glick.

all part of an international Satanic 'murder, drug smuggling, and child porno' cult. Because of this type of miseducation from the Christians, I feel Pagans *must* respond, or be prepared to go completely underground."

"There is just no place in this religion for a figure like Satan," Laurel said. "It's never even mentioned; the emphasis is so heavily on what is good and what would make you a better person, and what would bring you closer to your concept of God, whatever that happens to be. The big difference between Pagans and Christians or Jews or any other monotheistic religion is that Paganism gives you some scope to perceive your Deity as whatever you are comfortable perceiving Deity as. Is what I do so very different from a Roman Catholic praying to the Virgin Mary? No. I perceive God as being a Woman. And since I have been practicing Wicca, I have become much more conscious of my role in the world, as a citizen of this planet. I'm much more politically aware."

Mer-Nuit's daughter Tasha, age 12, wrote the following essay for a school assignment on what it means to be an American:

> I do not choose to be forced into the beliefs of others. It is my right to be my own person if I can. I seek independence . . . I want to be free to think my own thoughts, to say what I wish, and to exercise my constitutional right to do so. I refuse to be bullied by anyone . . . I prefer . . . the thrill of freedom to the dull calm of relative imprisonment. I will not trade this freedom for anything on earth, nor my own beliefs for those forced on me by others. I will never back off from this, nor will I allow my liberty to be taken away. It is my heritage to believe in myself and what I do, to respect the beliefs of others but not to be controlled by them, and to fight if necessary for my beliefs and say, this I have done. All this is what it means to me to be an American.

The police officer who organized the seminar at which Tara spoke is trying to make a difference in the way public officials view alternative spirituality. "People are suddenly saying, 'I have a right to openly worship the way I want to worship,' and they're coming out and they're coming into conflict with social service agencies, governmental agencies, and police departments that don't understand," he said. "It's simply a matter of them not understanding because they've been brought up under the influence of Judeo-Christian values and don't realize that the first amendment allows you to worship anybody—you could worship that doorknob if you wanted to." His course was designed to make government workers aware of the cultural and religious diversity of Americans. "People have an absolute right under the constitution to practice whatever religion they want, as long as they don't break the law of the land."

While Wiccans have not yet argued a case before the Supreme Court with regard to their religious beliefs, other minority religions have. The "free exercise" clause of the 1st Amendment was central to both *Employment Division of Oregon vs. Smith* (1990) and *Church of Lukumi Babalu Aye vs. City of Hialeah* (1993). In the Smith case, two men (both members of the Native American Church) lost their jobs because of their use of peyote in religious ceremonies, and were denied unemployment benefits by the State. The Supreme Court ruled in favor of Oregon, saying that states may make laws governing the use of drugs by their citizens and that the "free exercise" clause did not exempt the men from the law, as it applied to every citizen of the state—it was "generally applicable,"[9] and did not single out a specific group for restriction.

The principle of "general applicability" worked in favor of the Church of Lukumi Babalu Aye, a Santerian church. Soon after the Church leased an abandoned car lot with the intention of opening a place of worship in Hialeah, Florida, the city passed four ordinances prohibiting the killing of animals[10] in Santerian rituals. However, the city did not make laws against "the secular killing of animals, such as boiling live lobsters or hunting."[11] In early 1993, the Supreme Court ruled in favor of the Church, because a law had been written expressly to restrict members of the Church from the free exercise of their religion.

How might this "generally applicable" ruling affect Wiccans? One prediction is that conducting a public Skyclad ritual will land you in jail with no hope of invoking the 1st Amendment as a defense, whether or not it *is* your sincere religious belief. But if the city of Jonesboro, Arkansas, goes so far as to create an ordinance forbidding the sale of religious items by non-Christians, it will find itself arguing

---

[9] Neuman.
[10] "Ritual Sacrifice Poses Hazards, High Court Told," by Nancy Roman, THE WASHINGTON TIMES, Nov. 5, 1992.
[11] Neuman.

its case before the high court of the nation. However, until a case specifically addressing the civil rights of Wiccans is ruled upon by the Supreme Court, the most important thing any Pagan can do is stay informed, ready to defend herself and her fellow peaceful warriors in the struggle for recognition and protection.

Should you or your group become embroiled in a legal dispute, it is imperative that you retain competent legal representation as soon as possible. Get your story to the Pagan newsletters (see the resource appendix for addresses); plan a media campaign and get the news to cover your story; call the Unitarian Churches in your area and ask for support; use your network of contacts to get the word out in your area. And regardless of your political views, the American Civil Liberties Union should be contacted at the first sign of trouble over the right to practice the religion of your choice. In fact, thanks to ACLU support, the city of Chicago recently "waived a city liability insurance requirement so that Witches could dance in Grant Park under the Full Moon."[12]

And Pagans rally together in other parts of the country as well. In October of 1990, Texas Televangelist Larry Lea, a Pentecostal minister, declared a "Holy War" on the Pagans and homosexuals of the San Francisco Bay area. He gathered his "flock" inside a civic building for a revival that planned to take its mission to the streets; however, an estimated 50,000 Pagans and supporters surrounded the building in a peaceful protest—Lea never took his group outdoors.[13]

---

[12] "Postcards," American City & County, November 1993.
[13] Knight-Ridder News Service, October 27, 1990.

JOURNAL ENTRIES

1. How comfortable am I publicly confronting the stereotypes associated with Witches?

2. Would I participate in a demonstration against religious discrimination? What if I were at the center of such a protest—would I expect my friends to risk exposure in my defense?

3. When I think about Tara speaking to those law enforcement officers and social workers, I feel:

4. I think the police in my community would react this way to group/ Circle/Coven:

5. Do I feel safe from religious discrimination in my own community? my job? my home?

6. How many of my friends know about my religious beliefs? How comfortable am I sharing that part of myself with them?

COPPER KEY RECOMMENDS:

Fiction:

Stranger in a Strange Land, by Robert Heinlein; New York: G.P. Putnam's Sons, © 1961.

When God Was a Woman, by Merlin Stone; New York: Dial Press, ©1976.

For information on national Witches' organizations geared toward the promotion and protection of civil rights for Witches and Pagans, send a self-addressed stamped envelope to the following:

Witches' Anti-Discrimination Lobby
Dr. Leo Martello, H.P.
153 West 80 Street, Apt. 1B
New York, New York 10024

Witches' League for Public Awareness
Post Office Box 8736
Salem, Massachusetts 01970

Note: The American Civil Liberties Union has offices in most metropolitan areas; check your local phone directory or that of the nearest large city for the chapter which represents your area.

10
A YEAR PAST COVENSTEAD

FOXFIRE'S STORY

WISPY, BLACK clouds racing across the face of the Full Moon, the voice of the wind howling under the door, the smell of the damp Spring earth—even as a child, the faces and voices of Nature drew me to them. When the Moon lit my bedroom, I would get up and go to the window, following her mysterious light. I could feel the energy of a storm, its power, its unexplained and unleashed power.

For many years, I considered this strong attraction to the natural world as just another quirk in my personality. I'd always been a bit odd; I found it strange that other people could be so oblivious to the wonders of Mother Nature. To them, the natural world was merely scenery. It was to be enjoyed when it appeared friendly and avoided when it showed its wild and untamed side. I, however, relished the natural world in all its forms. To me, it was not something outside myself, but something of which I was a part.

Perhaps this love of the Moon and the darkness of the night was one of the reasons that early in my life, Halloween became my favorite holiday. Unlike other children, I didn't care that much for scary stories and trick-or-treat candy. There definitely was something magical about this night, but for me there was nothing frightening. I loved being out on Halloween, when the Moon was full and bright, or peeking through swiftly moving black clouds.

One Halloween night, when I was about eleven years old, I left the group of trick-or-treaters I was with and went to an abandoned stable that stood behind a Civil War-era mansion in the suburban Baltimore neighborhood where I lived. All alone in the darkness, I leaned against an old tree and slid down its rough trunk and sat on the scaly roots below. The Moon was hidden totally by clouds, and the leafless trees blew strongly. It was so quiet there, with only the voice of the wind filling the night. Then all at once the Moon, bright and powerful, appeared from behind the thick clouds. I cannot explain the sense of peace and power that surged through me that night. I felt connected not only to the Earth on which I was sitting, but to something far more primal and ancient. I knew then that there was something sacred about this night, and I knew that no matter where I was, on Halloween I had to get away from the festivities of the holiday and go into the darkness and be alone with the Moon, the wind, and the trees.

For each Halloween thereafter, I did so. In college, it got to be a joke among my friends. One year, my roommate went with me. Together we sat under some old apple trees in a very neglected cemetery in our college town. The Moon was bright that night, and my roommate also felt something like what I was feeling. She too felt some of the power of the night, although she suggested that because we were both Irish we were probably feeling the presence of Banshees.

Of course, I did not know it at the time, but she probably was right. Our Celtic ancestry may have played a part in the recognition that something magical was happening. It would be many years later before I understood the ancient roots of my family.

I was definitely Irish, with a hefty dose of Welsh and English, and I was raised an Episcopalian. I enjoyed going to church during my early years, but I did not like reading the Bible. My best friend, a Presbyterian, was always encouraging me to read the book, but no matter how hard I tried, I just didn't like most of it.

I did like the book of Matthew, especially the Sermon on the Mount, and Jesus was okay. What I could not accept was the entire concept of God the Father. I was most unimpressed. My own earthly father seemed a lot nicer and more mature. While God the Father was punishing everyone and acting like a tyrant, my own father was reading us stories and taking us sledding and to baseball games.

In spite of my dislike of the Bible, the Episcopalian services were all right because the more negative aspects of the Bible were not emphasized at our particular church. One Sunday, when I was about nine years old, as I was singing "Onward Christian Soldiers," the words just stuck in my throat and a horrible chill ran along my back. I could not finish the song, and I could never sing it again. The words were too horrible, and for some strange reason, they seemed very personal. Although I ended up getting confirmed, I stopped going to church as a teenager. And although there was something healing and spiritual when I was alone outdoors, particularly at night, I had not yet come to think of these times as particularly religious.

One day, years later, when I was living in a large, midwestern city, my husband suggested that we go to a Witches' bookstore that he had discovered on his lunch hour. I was horrified at the thought and urged him to avoid the place. Looking back, I find my reaction was strange for three reasons: I was not a Christian or a follower of any other religion, so why was I accepting the popular myth regarding Witchcraft? I was intellectually curious, so why was I not curious about this? Why did I actually believe there was a potential for power in that particular religion? I guess, like so many other people, I believed Witches were devil worshipers or dabbled in the occult in negative ways.

It was not until I read Mary Daly's book, *Gyn/Ecology*, that I started to see what Witchcraft really was about. Of all the books I have ever read, that one affected my life most. She revealed me to myself, expressing verbally the visceral things I already knew but could never articulate. Her chapter on the Witch burnings hit home with me, as did all the other chapters in her book. I had a hunger to know more about Witches; I sensed a homecoming.

While I slogged through many of the books footnoted in Daly's work, I still couldn't find much on Witchcraft. The local women's bookstore had some, but not many. One day, when my yoga teacher and our class were having lunch together, we passed the Witches bookstore and the teacher suggested we stop in, since it was one of her favorite places. Although I cannot say that I was as comfortable there as I was in the women's bookstore, I was absolutely fascinated by the abundance of books on Witches and the Craft.

We moved about this time, and for several years, I was unable to find any more books to satisfy my hunger for information about Witchcraft. Eventually, I ran across Adler's *Drawing Down the Moon*, and I knew then that I was home. It was so exciting to find others like myself in print, even if I did not know them in person. I was sure I wouldn't find any Witches in the city to which we had moved, but we weren't too far from a rather eclectic Lesbian commune. I went there to meet the women, and through them I discovered some who were worshiping the Goddess.

I'll never forget the short first ritual we all did together one summer evening. There were five of us who stood shoulder-to-shoulder in a Circle overlooking the lake on which I lived. We honored the four directions and thanked the Goddess by chanting. It was a short but powerful ritual. Throughout the summer when these women had time, we would swim together naked in the lake and talk about the Witches and Pagans of the past.

Eventually my new friends disappeared as the commune closed, and for several years I had no contact with Pagans. Every time I went out of town, I would explore bookstores in other cities and buy books on Wicca and feminism. After my divorce, I came across a group of Pagans in my area and celebrated my first Lughnasad with them. I enjoyed this group, but they occasionally did drugs, and I wasn't interested in that so I stopped meeting with them.

Throughout the years, in spite of the lack of Pagan community, I continued my bond with Nature, communing with the Full Moon, the trees, and the wind, and feeling the passion of storms. Since my house was in the country, I would take two or three of my German Shepherds and go out in the Moonlit fields on Halloween and feel the power of the night. Of course by this time I no longer called it Halloween but by its proper Celtic name, Samhain. Even after all the years of spending this night alone, I still felt the power of this special time. Often I would listen to Celtic harp music or the Chieftains before I would walk into the night. The music would send me back into that place where there are no words, only the recognition of something unspoken and ancient.

As my connection to my Celtic past grew, so did my feminism and my interest in Wicca. I subscribed to several Pagan magazines, and continued to devour every Pagan book I could find. Finally, some Pagan folk singers appeared at the Unitarian Church I had joined in search of a CUUPS chapter. The woman singer was scheduled to give a talk the following day at a newly opened women's bookstore. I decided to go—I was surprised and excited to learn that there was an interest in Wicca in my city. I talked to the owner of the bookstore who told me that a group of women was gathering to worship the Goddess.

I attended the first meeting, and was delighted to find such an eclectic and intelligent group of women. We sat in a small Circle with candles burning and incense filling the room. We were nervous, partly because we were strangers, and partly because we didn't know if we were doing things properly. But instinct and magic kicked in and we left that first Circle knowing that something special had been created and that we would continue to meet.

Copper Key has grown in a way that is difficult to describe. Although some members have left and new ones have come, a unique and powerful bond formed between the individuals in the group. Wicca has united us in a way that has led to a deep and vibrant sense of community. This awareness of community and this desire to incorporate Wicca into our daily lives has unleashed a powerful vortex of creativity among the members of the group.

As we live our day-to-day lives, we keep in close contact with one another, always aware that through Wicca we have been able to participate in this Coven that has become a source of love and celebration. Even when we socialize as a group, it is evident that there is some deep bond between the members of Copper Key. We spark a certain vibrant energy in one another, and there is the familiarity of women who are deeply devoted to one another and the Craft.

Although I may eventually move once more and leave behind the daily interaction with the members of Copper Key, I will still feel the presence of the group in my life. I see myself as carrying the seed of Copper Key within me, and wherever I go, I will be nourished by the love and sense of homecoming I've found within the Coven. Hopefully, there will be others out there with whom I will link, and together we can create another group that is empowered by the cycles of Wicca.

The many moods and faces of Nature continue to delight me, and while I still love being alone outdoors in the dark and I can still feel the primal energy of a storm, having a Coven to celebrate the seasons and passage of time has given me a unique sense of connection to others, both living and dead. Copper Key, while rooted firmly in the present, is also a legacy from the past, and I think each of us has not only a sense of knowing one another in another time, but also an acute awareness of our Pagan ancestors. This sense of not only the here and now but also the most ancient times creates a deep awareness and reverence in me, as well as a feeling of being intimately a part of life's infinite dance. That force that led me as a child out into the Moonlit darkness has come full circle now, as I join with my sisters in Copper Key to celebrate the Goddess, the seasons, and the cycles of birth, life, death, and rebirth. Like Copper Key itself, as a member of the Coven, I feel myself constantly being reborn.

MERRY MEET . . .

IN THE summer of 1992, Acacia's husband was offered a professorship at a university in another city. She had known for some time of the possibility of her moving, and Copper Key had known as well.

The farewell Circle they cast included the owner of the bookstore where the Coven first met. Tara and Laurel served as Priestesses. Each member brought Acacia a gift to remember them by—a book from Foxfire, scented oil from River, hand-carved Runes from Branwen, a blank journal from Ivy, a butterfly from Tara, moon, sun and stars pins from Mer-Nuit, a bottle shaped like the Venus of Willendorf from Ginger, a slice of blue agate from Orchid, a gris-gris from the bookstore, a hand-made crescent moon from Hannah, a painted rock from Laurel, and chocolate fudge from Sabina.

During the Work of the Circle, Laurel wove red yarn, which had been hand-carded, spun, and dyed, around the waists of all the women in the group, and the women in turn passed the skein back and forth over the center of the Altar until a red web of yarn held the women together. During the weaving, the women sang, "She changes everything She touches, and everything She touches changes"[1] and "We are the flow, we are the ebb, we are the weavers, we are the web."[2]

"We stood all together, and we were all holding a piece of the web, and my hand was tingling, there was so much energy coming

---

[1] *The Kore Chant,* by Starhawk & Lauren Liebling; CHANTS: Ritual Music of the Reclaiming Community. To order the tape, write: Reclaiming Chants, Post Office Box 14404, San Francisco, California, 94114.
[2] *We are the Flow,* by Shekinah Mountainwater; ibid.

through that yarn," Laurel said. "Acacia's good-bye Circle was one of the ones I consider the most moving for me personally that year."

After the Priestesses felt that the energy had reached its peak, the Athame was passed, and the strands were cut around each individual; they took the yarn home for their individual shrines. Tara also wrapped up the altar cloth for Acacia to take to her new home.

"I have not found a group like Copper Key, although I have met some terrific people among the Pagans of our new city," Acacia said, nearly a year after the move. "It may be that there is no way to experience the kind of community I had with Copper Key because, from here on, I am the newcomer to any Circle. It could be that it just takes a long time to hook up again. I trust that I am walking the path to which I am constantly called, and I do believe there is a reason for this part of my life. I may not be completely thrilled about the experience, but I have faith that there is something to be learned."

. . . AND MERRY PART . . .

NEARLY NINE months after Acacia's good-bye, Laurel called a meeting with Copper Key to announce that she was leaving the Circle to practice the Craft as a Solitary. Her reasons for leaving and how she felt a few months after her departure are below, in her own words:

"The decision to leave took a long time to evolve . . . I didn't just wake up one day, and say, 'Oh, I think I'll leave Copper Key.' The idea would come and sometimes I would feel very definitely that I should leave. Then it would recede and I'd think I should stay. Finally, I reached the point where the high tides saying I should leave were coming much more frequent than the low tides saying I should stay. My decision to leave was based on one reason: It was time for me to move on to a different level of working.

"When we first began meeting, we were very focused on ritual. We had to be; none of us had ever been in a Circle before. The mechanics of getting through the ritual were completely absorbing. We did very little work in the Circle because it was exhausting just getting through the whole thing in the right order. Gradually, we gained basic skills and began to move away from that a little, but not fast enough as far as I was concerned. I had reached the point where the ritual was just the mechanics and the Work of the Circle was terribly important. The newer members were still in the phase of learning how to do ritual and learning what was important about ritual for them. The work that we were doing as a Coven was not the work that I needed to be doing for my *own* furtherance in my Craft studies.

"I felt that I had already attained a certain level of power and ability in creating a ritual space; true, I'm not the most suave, smoothest Priestess on Earth, but I have a feeling for what ritual is supposed to accomplish, and I can do it a lot more expediently and with a lot less red tape just working alone. I can achieve the same sense of concentration and exclusion of the mundane world just by meditating. I can do the whole thing in my mind, and not have to get up and walk around or set up a whole lot of paraphernalia. But I do think everyone has to go through learning how to do ritual before they can move out on their own.

"Basically, I believe Wicca is a solitary path, and at some point almost everyone will feel like they need to work alone for a time.

"I would eventually like to work again with at least three or so people to whom I could say anything, without having to weigh it and decide how they might deal with it or interpret it. But that is not my focus right now.

"I am still studying with Hidden Grove. I have advanced in that system, but like most elevations, it occurred after the fact. If you have moved to a deeper level of knowing and accepting yourself, and understanding what gifts you have and how to use them to honor the Gods, then you have moved closer to the middle of that onion, which is a good analogy for that process. You don't really need anyone to tell you that you have progressed, but it's nice to have a ritual to commemorate the fact that you've moved on. I don't meet with the Hidden Grove people regularly, because they live in different cities, but I do still study their material and communicate with certain of their initiates on a regular basis.

"With Copper Key, there was a real sense at one time of community and companionship and of starting out on a great adventure together. It was really exciting. We were going to a place that none of us had ever been, and we were going together. It created bonds that have continued since I left Copper Key; some of the best friends that I have are women I did not know before that group was organized. I still have a warm spot in my heart for the ones I don't talk to on a regular basis. We shared a lot. The community, the sharing, the network, and the support of twelve other women are the things I miss."

. . . AND MERRY MEET AGAIN

DID ACACIA'S moving away or Laurel's leaving mean the end of the Coven? No; the next generation of Copper Key is busy learning what it means to create community.

Through Mer-Nuit's efforts to start a CUUPS chapter at the local Unitarian Universalist Church, Willow met some of the members of Copper Key. After she was involved helping the fledgling CUUPS chapter plan events, the members extended her an invitation to an open Circle.Once she had spent a few Lunar cycles with them, they asked her to spend the next year-and-a-day discovering whether she belonged to the Coven. She accepted.

Willow was among the group from Copper Key that attended the public demonstration against the closing of an "occult" shop by the Religious Right. When asked about going public, she said, "I felt the 1st Amendment was at risk—and still is. When I was a child, the Ku Klux Klan burned a cross in the yard of the Catholic church my family attended. We left town for over a month or so. As an adult, I feel that people with some job security need to stand up to help those who can't take the risk of exposure. It is very important for me not to be confined to the 'broom closet'. . ."

Willow is the first new member to Copper Key since Acacia's farewell Circle in the Autumn of 1992. The Coven now sits with an open space when doing ritual, hoping that the Goddess will send a woman their way who will weave the Web in Laurel's absence. If the first three years are any indication, they won't be waiting long.

JOURNAL ENTRIES

1. How have I dealt with friends moving away in the past? What feelings stir within me when I think about a close friend leaving?

2. Would I be able to leave a Circle of friends if I felt that I needed to be working on a different level?

3. Foxfire's story struck these chords in me:

4. How well do I deal with change?

5. Will I be comfortable welcoming new people into my Circle? Would I be comfortable during a chance meeting with a member who has left my Circle?

COPPER KEY RECOMMENDS:

Gyn/Ecology, by Mary Daly; Boston, Massachusetts: The Beacon Press, ©1978.

GROUP
EXERCISES

FIRST MEETING ICEBREAKER

AT THE first meeting of your Circle, there is bound to be a little nervous tension running around. If you are the leader or Priestess for the evening, that tension is bound to make it even harder on you. The most important thing you can do is to involve the group in an exercise that takes you out of the spotlight and makes each member of the group a focal point.

For this exercise, you will need a large hat (or a box or bowl), and three different colors of confetti. The confetti can be purchased at a party or hobby store, or you can make some yourself with a hole puncher and colored paper. Whatever you choose to use, you should gather a fairly large supply—enough for each member of the meeting to take a small handful.

Mix the three colors up in the hat. Pass the hat around high over the heads of the group and ask them to reach in and grab some—let them determine how much or how little. After everyone (including you) has their confetti, explain that each of them will now be asked to share things about themselves based on the color and number of their confetti.

For example, decide that the red confetti stands for something about the person's background—their birthday, the type of work they do, the number of children they may have, their hobbies. Blue could be for their religious background—what churches they may have attended as children, what traditions they have studied among the Pagan faiths, what path they feel called to now, a particular affinity they may have for a certain Goddess or God. Make yellow represent their likes and dislikes—favorite foods, favorite colors, whether they have pets, like camping, or would love to visit Paris. You may even want to take into account the types of things to be shared as you plan to mix the confetti—maybe more of the red and yellow than the blue.

As the instigator of this exercise, it is probably best that you start things off. This will give them an idea of what you expect from the exercise, and give them time to think a little about what they will say. If anyone seems uncomfortable, let her pass and then come back to her at the end.

After the exercise is over, encourage them to take the confetti home and decorate their personal shrine or a windowsill with it. You may want to open the next meeting with a spin-off exercise: go around the Circle, and for each person let the group shout out things about her that they remember from the first meeting.

THE TROUBLE WITH ORAL TRADITION

TAKE A poll in your group — how many people have ever played "Gossip," where a phrase or statement is passed around from one person to the other until the person at the end has to say out loud what they heard? This is an excellent way to introduce questions about oral tradition, or how elements of religions are handed down from generation to generation. Particularly in Pagan traditions, where so much of what is considered the "right" way to do things is in very few instances written down, certain practices, tenets of faith, or even ritual elements may seem quite strange to newcomers. Playing "Gossip" may help them understand how things came to be as they are.

Below are some sample phrases that you can "pass" in the Circle. An added bonus: at the end of each round, ask them to guess the source of the phrase (all are from sources which were originally oral traditions).

- The Moon it is that signals the feasts, a luminary that wanes after her full. *(Ecclesiasticus, 43:7 – The Old Testament)*

- You will never manage to deal equitably with women, no matter how hard   you try. *(The Quran, 4:129)*

- And they feed the women upon the flesh of their husbands, and the children upon the flesh of their fathers. *(Moroni, 9:8 – The Book of Mormon)*

- For that wonderful beauty, for that cunning witch, who enslaved nations by her debauchery, and tribes by her spells. *(Nahum, 3:4 – The Old Testament)*

GETTING TO KNOW YOUR CIRCLE: THE SURVEY EXERCISE

THE GOAL of the Survey Exercise is to provide a vehicle for your Circle to discuss some very specific issues which may affect the way the group interacts, the way they worship together, and the things they wish to study. You may also discover that some members have mastered particular skills which they are willing to share with the group, such as astrology or growing herbs. The survey form is broken into three sections, each with a specific focus. These pages are perforated so that they may be removed from the book and copied for your group.

It is recommended that you set aside at least an hour for each of the three parts. Enough time must be allowed for members of the group to mark their responses, and also for the group to discuss the individual questions thoroughly. You may wish to complete the entire exercise over three meetings in the group time following ritual, or you may set aside a piece of an extended retreat to do the entire exercise. Each person must feel that s/he can voice honest opinions, concerns, and interests without judgment and without being "cut off" due to time.

Make sure you have enough copies of the survey and pens/pencils for everyone present. Allow the group to spread out to complete the inventory if they wish. When you call time, the group should reconvene in a circle and, starting with you, provide their answer to each question. After all have answered, open the floor for discussion. You may wish to remind the group that perfect love, perfect trust, and respect for each individual are crucial to becoming a working Coven.

The first part of the survey allows each member to explore the way that member practices the Craft. Some of the issues addressed, especially concerning the degree to which each member is "out of the broom closet," are fundamental to the smooth interaction of your group and the personal safety of each member. Also, specific elements of Wicca, such as practicing Skyclad, can be discussed openly and honestly in this framework.

Part II is simply titled "Beliefs," and deals with some topics that the general public would classify as "occult." Knowing how the members of your Circle feel about some of these issues may help facilitate the planning of future meetings and also allow members to let the group know those issues with which they feel comfortable and those with which they would not want to be involved.

Even those things which you *think* you know about each member should not be taken for granted. Part III of the survey asks members to expose such things as their age, their marital status, their religious background, their political affiliation, and their sexual orientation, among others.

Throughout the exercise, it is important to allow members to choose not to voice their answers out loud to the group. The ground rules should be discussed at the beginning of the exercise; your group may agree to voice their answers to every question, to turn in the survey anonymously to one person to tabulate the results and discuss them at a later date, or to keep their surveys and only offer answers to the questions which they choose. Even though the women of Copper Key filled out this inventory after they had been meeting for over a year, many were surprised by the results! If even one person in your Circle is uncomfortable with answering these questions, you would be better served to let some time pass and then present the idea again.

At the time of Covenstead, twelve members of Copper Key were present and agreed to fill out the survey. Their responses are provided for you in each section, and any comments they had to make about the questions or the specific topics are listed as well.

If your group would like to share its information with others around the country, send a copy of your final tally sheet to the author in care of the publisher. You may attach additional sheets as necessary.

SURVEY PART I:

PRACTICE

1. Do you consider yourself a Witch?   Y   N

2. Do you consider yourself a Pagan?   Y   N

3. Have you participated in a ceremony or ritual that has
   committed you to Wicca?   Y   N

4. Have you ever practiced Wicca Skyclad (ritually nude)?

                                                   Y   N

5. Have you ever cast a spell?   Y   N

6. Do you make New Moon vows?   Y   N

   How effective have these vows been in modifying your behavior?
   Very Effective 1 2 3 4 5 No Change

7. Do you make Full Moon wishes?   Y   N

   How frequently do these wishes come true?
   Often 1 2 3 4 5 Never

8. Have you had "mystical" experiences either in or out of ritual?

                                                   Y   N
   Briefly explain: _____

   _____

   _____

   _____

   _____

9. Have you ever seen or been a party to a ritual which involved sexual intercourse?

                                                   Y   N

10. Do you believe in the Law of Three (that whatever you do comes back to you threefold)?

                                                   Y   N

Does this belief govern your actions as a Pagan?

                                                   Y   N

11. What effect has the practice of Wicca had on your life?
Positive 1 2 3 4 5 Negative

12. Have you lost friends or lovers because of your religious beliefs?

                                                   Y   N

13. To what extent are you "out of the broom closet"? (Who knows about your beliefs & practices?) Circle those that apply:

Community at large
Employer
Spouse
Children
Family of Origin
Other friends

Comments: Please note the question (i.e., 1,2,3) and put your comments here:

_____

_____

_____

_____

_____

PRACTICE OF THE CRAFT & COPPER KEY

1. DO YOU CONSIDER YOURSELF A WITCH?

Yes	No
11	1

"All Witches are Pagans but not all Pagans are Witches. In one group with which I work I consider myself a Witch. In another group, I am working toward becoming a Witch, but I have to earn the title."

"Yes, I consider myself a Witch. I practice a Wiccan path; what else would I call myself?"

"By Starhawk's definition I am a Witch: I am wild. I am free. I am woman. I am Witch."

2. DO YOU CONSIDER YOURSELF A PAGAN?

Yes	No
12	0

"I am definitely a Pagan. I cannot stand the idea of being a Christian hypocrite. I believe Nature was here before me and is to be revered as an inhabitant of Earth. As for the part of me that is both God & Goddess, I have existed since the beginning of time."

"I consider myself a Pagan in terms which mean I am not a Christian nor do I hold a Christian world view."

3. HAVE YOU PARTICIPATED IN A CEREMONY OR RITUAL THAT HAS COMMITTED YOU TO WICCA?

Yes	No
9	3

"Basically, I have been Pagan my whole life—even when I went to the Baptist church with family I had my own ideas. I have always been interested in what is little known about, such as the mysteries of divination. When I was young, I had 'magical jewelry.' I started practicing solitary and eventually connected with my working groups."

"I took dedication in a formal ceremony approximately one year ago. The dedication was a vow to study in its narrow sense but it was a recognition that I am a Witch and a commitment to follow a Wiccan Path as I see it. I have taken 'Covenstead' but because my group is non-hierarchal in structure there is no one to initiate us into the Craft. It's an interesting issue."

4. HAVE YOU EVER PRACTICED WICCA SKYCLAD (RITUALLY NUDE)?

Yes	No
7	5

5. HAVE YOU EVER CAST A SPELL?

Yes	No
11	1

6. DO YOU MAKE NEW MOON VOWS?

Yes	No
12	0

HOW EFFECTIVE HAVE THESE VOWS BEEN IN MODIFYING YOUR BEHAVIOR?

Very Effective	Mid-Range	No Change
8	3	1

7. DO YOU MAKE FULL MOON WISHES?

Yes	No
12	0

HOW FREQUENTLY DO THESE WISHES COME TRUE?

Often	Mid-range	Never
4	8	0

8. HAVE YOU HAD "MYSTICAL" EXPERIENCES EITHER IN OR OUT OF RITUAL? (Please briefly explain)

Yes	No
11	1

"At a ritual where there was a drawing down, I really connected and felt particularly empowered, more so than I had ever before."

"Quite often during sex with my fiance; once on a boat in the middle of the ocean at night when phosphorescent creatures were floating in the water; during drawing downs (witnessing it the first time especially); other times too."

"I do a lot of philosophical soul-searching, and I feel that I know the answers to everything—the secrets of the universe—but that somehow they are repressed—intentionally—so that I have to learn them as I go."

"Everything is mystical if you take the time to notice. The most significant experience that has occurred to me was in a ritual when I was by myself and I attempted a drawing down. There were physical feelings that were very real!"

"Prophetic dreams, visions, heard voices, had premonitions."

"I have had a dream of ritual marriage—very positive, very powerful. Many experiences of synchronicity; Goddess experiences—too much to write!"

"Past life remembrances and recognition of people I've just met as being known before."

"Sometimes see auras; experienced telepathy."

9. HAVE YOU EVER SEEN OR BEEN PARTY TO A RITUAL WHICH INVOLVED SEXUAL INTERCOURSE?

Yes	No
0	12

10. DO YOU BELIEVE IN THE LAW OF THREE?

Yes	No
11	1

DOES THIS BELIEF GOVERN YOUR ACTIONS AS A PAGAN?

Yes	No	"Somewhat"
10	1	1

11. WHAT EFFECT HAS THE PRACTICE OF WICCA HAD ON YOUR LIFE?

Positive	Midrange	Negative
11	1	0

12. HAVE YOU LOST FRIENDS OR LOVERS BECAUSE OF YOUR RELIGIOUS BELIEFS?

Yes	No
4	8

13. TO WHAT EXTENT ARE YOU "OUT OF THE BROOM CLOSET" (WHO KNOWS ABOUT YOUR BELIEFS AND PRACTICES?)

Community at Large:	3
Employer:	2
Spouse:	6
Children:	6
Family of Origin:	5
Other friends:	11

"I am very committed to being out of the closet. I am fortunate to be in a position to be open. I hope that by being open, I can maybe expose people to our way of life as a positive, caring path, so maybe those people who can't be 'out' one day can be if they choose to be. I also feel that since I can be open, by not being so I would be implying that something is wrong with Paganism, that I have something to hide. I am not pushy, I don't encourage people to come to Circle unless they ask. Someone has to speak up for us and very few non-Pagans will unless they know one of us. By being open, I can also provide a point of contact with the Pagan community for those who need one."

SURVEY PART II:

BELIEFS

Circle the number that best applies:

A. Reincarnation:
    Strongly Believe 1 2 3 4 5 Don't Believe

B. Magical Properties of Herbs:
    Strongly Believe 1 2 3 4 5 Don't Believe

C. Spells for Personal Growth:
    Strongly Believe 1 2 3 4 5 Don't Believe

D. Spells to Bind Others:
    Strongly Believe 1 2 3 4 5 Don't Believe

E. Polytheism:
    Strongly Believe 1 2 3 4 5 Don't Believe

F. Female Deity/Goddess:
    Strongly Believe 1 2 3 4 5 Don't Believe

G. Male Deity/God:
    Strongly Believe 1 2 3 4 5 Don't Believe

H. Drawing Down:
    Strongly Believe 1 2 3 4 5 Don't Believe

I. Channeling:
    Strongly Believe 1 2 3 4 5 Don't Believe

J. Divination (i.e., Tarot, Scrying, Runes, etc.):
    Strongly Believe 1 2 3 4 5 Don't Believe

K. Astrology:
    Strongly Believe 1 2 3 4 5 Don't Believe

L. Elemental Spirits/Watchtowers:
   Strongly Believe 1 2 3 4 5 Don't Believe

M. Telepathy:
   Strongly Believe 1 2 3 4 5 Don't Believe

N. Astral Projection:
   Strongly Believe 1 2 3 4 5 Don't Believe

O. Precognition:
   Strongly Believe 1 2 3 4 5 Don't Believe

P. Auras:
   Strongly Believe 1 2 3 4 5 Don't Believe

Q. Faith Healing:
   Strongly Believe 1 2 3 4 5 Don't Believe

R. Evil and Benign Spirits:
   Strongly Believe 1 2 3 4 5 Don't Believe

S. Gaia Theory/Living Planet:
   Strongly Believe 1 2 3 4 5 Don't Believe

T. Numerology:
   Strongly Believe 1 2 3 4 5 Don't Believe

U. Palmistry:
   Strongly Believe 1 2 3 4 5 Don't Believe

V. Energy Properties of Crystals:
   Strongly Believe 1 2 3 4 5 Don't Believe

W. Witches:
   Strongly Believe 1 2 3 4 5 Don't Believe

X. Cones of Power:
Strongly Believe 1 2 3 4 5 Don't Believe

Y. Familiars:
Strongly Believe 1 2 3 4 5 Don't Believe

Z. Lunar Cycles of Energy:
Strongly Believe 1 2 3 4 5 Don't Believe

Comments: Please note the item (i.e., A, B, C) and put your comments here: _____

_____

_____

_____

BELIEFS OF COPPER KEY

A. REINCARNATION:

Strongly Believe	Mid-Range	Don't Believe
6	6	0

"I believe that each life serves to teach certain messages to each individual which lead to their personal, spiritual growth, and eventually leads to the culmination of the spirits."

"I believe in reincarnation in the sense that everything is a part of the one: that is, everything is sacred, from trees to imagination to water to stars. Life is a continuum, a pulsation like a light switch: on/off, life/death. The opposite is the reason for the other pole's existence."

"I have moved very rapidly over the past two years from a belief that when they put pennies on your eyes it is the final moment for us all to a certainty that reincarnation is real. As a group, we watched The Burning Times. The dialogue says something to the effect that the burning times not only killed those women but that it destroyed what they knew. Everyone in the group softly said, 'I know.' I am certain I know what they knew."

B. MAGICAL PROPERTIES OF HERBS:

Strongly Believe	Mid-Range	Don't Believe
5	7	0

"Herbs are the same as me, only composed differently. Just as some people are better at some things than others, or acquire skills that others do not, herbs have different 'skills.' Also, (when using herbs) we 'will' the property into the herb."

"I have no real experience with this issue, but based on my world view, I remain 'open' to that possibility."

"Drugs alone will not heal, but when introduced into a body they become healing tools. Herbs may act in a similar fashion."

C. SPELLS FOR PERSONAL GROWTH:

Strongly Believe	Mid-Range	Don't Believe
8	4	0

"I believe in all spells. If a person truly believes in what s/he is doing, that is all the proof one needs. If the person who performs the spell believes it, that's it. Personal growth is a personal thing."

"Spells are a focused act of WILL. Anyone who has gone through therapy knows the reality of change possible and that that process of change consists of altering yourself and your world views and a decision to allow change. A spell by any other name . . . "

D. SPELLS TO BIND OTHERS:

Strongly Believe	Mid-Range	Don't Believe
3	5	4

"I do not believe that spells to bind others are ethical."

"I believe this screws up your karma."

"I have a strong faith in the power of free will."

E. POLYTHEISM:

Strongly Believe	Mid-Range	Don't Believe	No Response
7	4	0	1

F. FEMALE DEITY/GODDESS:

Strongly Believe	Mid-Range	Don't Believe
9	3	0

G. MALE DEITY/GOD:

Strongly Believe	Mid-Range	Don't Believe	"Don't Care"
5	5	1	1

H. DRAWING DOWN:

Strongly Believe	Mid-Range	Don't Believe
8	4	0

"Entertaining or hosting another personality or entity in a consciousness is certainly possible . . . the prospect of drawing down both frightens and entices me."

I. CHANNELING:

Strongly Believe	Mid-Range	Don't Believe
1	11	0

"This is distinguished from 'drawing down' in that the entity is not divine but rather some waif spirit. I am more skeptical of this . . . the channeling I have witnessed was tied to the host's profession and income."

J. DIVINATION (i.e., Tarot, Scrying, Runes, etc.):

Strongly Believe	Mid-Range	Don't Believe
5	7	0

"The validity . . . has a psychological basis in allowing the subconscious to provide imagination and creativity in problem solving."

K. ASTROLOGY:

Strongly Believe	Mid-Range	Don't Believe
3	8	1

"My experience is that there are certain times when things are more easily accomplished—moon phases and seasons of the year. I am open to the possibility that the position of the planets is a factor."

L. ELEMENTAL SPIRITS/WATCHTOWERS:

Strongly Believe	Mid-Range	Don't Believe
6	6	0

"I have had direct experience in drawing them down, and they were my first encounter with mystical experience."

M. TELEPATHY:

Strongly Believe	Mid-Range	Don't Believe
9	3	0

N. ASTRAL PROJECTION:

Strongly Believe	Mid-Range	Don't Believe
9	3	0

O. PRECOGNITION:

Strongly Believe	Mid-Range	Don't Believe
10	2	0

P. AURAS:

Strongly Believe	Mid-Range	Don't Believe
6	6	0

Q. FAITH HEALING:

Strongly Believe	Mid-Range	Don't Believe
7	5	0

"As far as faith healing, I mean for myself, not for or towards others."

"What kind of faith healing? Our kind, I strongly believe in; Jimmy Swaggart's kind I don't believe in."

"As Starhawk points out, a spell is no substitute for an antibiotic, but I have had a 'healing' experience."

"I have seen cancer patients ease their pain with mental imaging, and I have personally used imaging to get rid of nausea during chemotherapy. I have been to groups that used reiki, accupressure, and even psychic surgery. The most successful healing I have seen involves a person who comes to Circle with a specific problem, asks for the Circle's energy and prayers, and works to take care of herself."

R. EVIL AND BENIGN SPIRITS:

Strongly Believe	Mid-Range	Don't Believe
6	4	2

"I believe in the phenomena of evil spirits but don't know what the real explanation is."

"I do not believe in the existence of evil, period."

"Spirits *are*—good and evil are our projections."

"I do not think evil behavior is caused by invasion of a sentient being of impure intent—the devil didn't make you do it, you have choice."

"The closest concept to the Christian good vs. evil dualism in Paganism is the idea of creativity & harmony vs. a non-creative & destructive idea which disconnects you from the Web. The idea of assigning a Christian value to a Pagan sense of spirit is difficult."

S. GAIA THEORY/LIVING PLANET:

Strongly Believe	Mid-Range	Don't Believe
11	1	0

"In the short time I have practiced the Craft, I have felt such a connection to the Earth that I now recognize it as a whole living entity. It is so profoundly spiritual that it is difficult to apply logic to the concept."

T. NUMEROLOGY:

Strongly Believe	Mid-Range	Don't Believe	No Response
1	6	3	1

"The magic is in the doer, not the instrument."

U. PALMISTRY:

Strongly Believe	Mid-Range	Don't Believe
1	10	1

"Maybe I just haven't met a good palmist."

V. ENERGY PROPERTIES OF CRYSTALS:

Strongly Believe	Mid-Range	Don't Believe
2	10	0

"Same as the magical properties of herbs."

"I do not believe that strip-mining the Earth to collect minerals is a very smart way to live in a nature religion like Wicca. However, occasionally you find a special rock on the road or in the woods which might help you feel more connected if you put it on your shrine or carry it in your pocket. As long as you leave a libation in return, you have stayed 'on the path'."

W. WITCHES:

Strongly Believe	Mid-Range	Don't Believe
12	0	0

X. CONES OF POWER:

Strongly Believe	Mid-Range	Don't Believe
9	3	0

"In my experience, the energy certainly goes somewhere."

Y. FAMILIARS:

Strongly Believe	Mid-Range	Don't Believe
3	8	1

"This is a Christian concept connected with the idea of Satan. Since I don't recognize the Devil or Hell, I can't fit this idea into my view."

"I don't believe animals do our bidding, but I do believe that animals are very sensitive to people and energies. One legend has it that cats will not go anywhere that evil is being practiced—I have three who enjoy being right in the middle of our Circles."

Z. LUNAR CYCLES OF ENERGY:

Strongly Believe	Mid-Range	Don't Believe
9	3	0

General comment on "Beliefs" portion of the inventory:

"Most of the things I marked 'strongly believe' I have witnessed or, as in the case of the Gods, have personal meaning for me. As far as spells—well, maybe they work and maybe they don't. All I can say is that sometimes the coincidence is too specific or too 'spooky,' and you get a feeling that makes your hair stand on end, but not entirely in a bad way. I believe it, and that's all I have the right or need to say."

SURVEY PART III:

DEMOGRAPHIC COMPOSITION OF YOUR COVEN:

Age:
Gender:
Ethnicity:
Marital Status:
Number of Offspring:
Sexual Orientation:
Education:
Profession:
Dietary Practice:
Religious Heritage:
Political Affiliation:

Please rank the following political issues from 1 to 7, 1 being the issue which occupies the most amount of your personal time, energy, and/ or money and 7 occupying the least:

_____ Feminism/Gender Equality
_____ Environmentalism
_____ 1st Amendment Issues (i.e., Freedom of Religion)
_____ Abortion Rights
_____ World Peace
_____ Animal Rights
_____ Homelessness

DEMOGRAPHIC COMPOSITION OF COPPER KEY

1. AGE:

22 - 30	31 - 40	41 - 50
4	3	5

2. GENDER:

F	M
12	0

3. ETHNICITY: All thirteen of the Coven members would be considered Caucasian or European-American in a standard survey. Their actual answers are listed below, in alphabetical order:

Anglo
Anglo-Italian
Caucasian (2)
Celtic, British, Dutch
English, German
German, Am. Indian
Irish, Welsh, English
Italian, Irish, Scotch
"Melting Pot" — Irish, English, Dutch, German, Am. Indian
Miscellaneous

4. MARITAL STATUS:

Married	Divorced	Single
6	3	3

5. NUMBER OF CHILDREN:

None	1-3	4+
5	6	1

6. SEXUAL ORIENTATION:

Heterosexual	Lesbian	Bisexual	No Response
7	1	3	1

7. EDUCATIONAL LEVEL:

Adv. Degree	College Degree	Some College	H.S. Diploma
2	7	2	1

8. PROFESSION: Many of the group felt that the role of parent was on par with or exceeded the duty of earning a living, and the list below reflects one who listed Mother before her society-recognized career. Additionally, one respondent wrote:

"Feminist first and foremost, but I earn money from the patriarchy as a legal secretary." Point made and taken by the author. Responses are listed below, in alphabetical order:

Artist	Editor	Sales
Attorney	Legal Secretary	Student (2)
City Planner	Mother	Waiter
College Instructor	Museum Professional	Writer

9. DIETARY PRACTICE:

Omnivore	Vegetarian
11	1

10. RELIGIOUS HERITAGE, actual responses in alphabetical order:

Baptist
Baptist & Catholic
Catholic (2)
Episcopalian (3)
Lutheran
Non-Denominational
"Not much of any"
Unitarian (2)

11. POLITICAL AFFILIATION:

Democrat	Republican	Independent
7	1	4

12. POLITICAL ISSUES: There was general grousing about this question as each woman got to it, and comments such as "it's too hard to rank these—I care about all of them" were heard over and over.

#1: Six of the women marked a "1" next to Feminism/Gender Equality; two marked Environmentalism; one each for 1st Amendment Issues, Abortion Rights, Animal Rights, and Homelessness.

#2: Five women ranked Abortion Rights "2"; four Feminism/Gender Equality; two Environmentalism; one 1st Amendment Issues.

#3: Four for 1st Amendment Issues; three for Abortion Rights; two for Environmentalism; one for Feminism/Gender Equality; one for World Peace.

CIRCLE NAMES MEDITATION

FINDING A Craft or Circle name may be as much an initiation as a formal dedication ceremony, or it might simply come to you in a dream. When your Coven participates in finding their individual names together, you build yet another bridge to one another. By planning to select names at a particular meeting, you also insure that no one in the group feels left behind.

The exercise will take a bit of preparation on the part of the entire group, and especially on the part of the Priestess for the night. Members of the Circle should research at least three names that they are drawn to—many books, such as *The Witches' Goddess*, provide an index of mythological names from around the world, and a book on wildflowers or wildlife from your own region of the country might be helpful. Once they have located three potential names, they should write them on three scraps of paper (one name per scrap) and bring them to the meeting.

In this modern world, electronics are aiding nature religions—it might seem incongruous to use a tape recorder to lead a meditation, but it certainly allows that every member of the group can participate. The Priestess should record at least fifteen minutes or more of a slow, steady, heart-beat rhythm on a drum, making sure that the beginning of the tape is a little faster than the middle, and that from the middle the beat gets progressively a little faster until it matches a regular, seated-position rate before it ends. This will help take the members of the group down to a meditative level and then bring them slowly out of it.

The meditation itself should take place *within the established ritual circle;* and you may wish to cast a little larger area than normal so that everyone may lie out flat within its confines. The best time to do this is during the Work of the Circle, probably the last work of the evening. The Priestess should set up what each person should be concentrating on before she turns on the tape, and let them know how long the meditation will last. Again, this will free her to participate as well.

Using a classic shamanic-type meditation as a framework for this work, the Priestess may select to use a cave, a forest, a house, or some other image into which the Coven members can concentrate on traveling. In the cave example, each member should see the path leading to the cave and follow it; see the mouth of the cave and enter it; follow a path in the cave down to an open chamber. The Priestess can add descriptions of the path and the rock and the stalactites and stalagmites to help them along. Once in the open chamber, they are to visualize the three scraps of paper (which they should actually be holding in their hands) lying facedown upon a flat rock in the center. In the house, this might be a table or a hearthstone; in the forest this could be a tree stump. They should imagine sitting in front of the table rock facing it; then pick up one scrap of paper, without looking at the name. Next, they should close their eyes in the cave or look at a blank wall and see what images come, hopefully from the association of the name on the paper which they hold. After picking up all three and seeing what is associated with each, they will decide which one feels the best or seems to suit them. They then turn that scrap of paper over, and see their name.

The Priestess should also tell the Coven members how to get back—following the same path out that they followed in, with the suggestion that it will be very simple to do, that there will be no trouble finding one's way. After the tape has finished, each person should relay their experience to the Coven and introduce themselves to their Circle.

NAMES OF COPPER KEY & FAMILY

FROM MYTHOLOGY:

Branwen:	Welsh devotee of Rhiannon
Diana:	Roman equivalent of the Greek Artemis
Mer-Nuit:	Egyptian Goddess
Tara:	Hindu Star Goddess, represents cycles and change: "Because I believe life is for joy, and that you can't be worried all the time about what comes next, I was drawn to her."

FROM NATURE:

Acacia

Briar

Foxfire — Saw a fox on three nights; Tara suggested the name

Ivy

Jade

Laurel

Moriah — The wind

Orchid — "I've always liked purple orchids, they're my favorite flower. The first time I was invited to a Circle, I felt this urge to bring something. I kept thinking I would find some orchids to bring, but I never made it to the florist. Finally, I realized that I was bringing myself to the Circle, and that I was the gift."

River

Seal

Wild Ginger — Reddish-brown flower, the root used in folk remedies for easing pregnancy and childbirth

OTHER:

Hannah — "It was the name I thought of myself as when I was a child. I decided that entering the Craft was starting a new life, and I wanted to keep and preserve that child part of me."

Maroona

Sabina

Tasha

NEWSLETTERS

Ambrosia, published by Brigit & Copernicus of Earth Family, published Sabbatly; Post Office Box 212, Springfield, Missouri, 65801-0212.

Circle Network News, published by Selena Fox and the Circle Sanctuary; Box 219, Mount Horeb, Wisconsin, 53572.

Green Egg (adult Pagans) and *Ham* (for young Pagans and children of Pagans), published by the Church of All Worlds; Post Office Box 212, Redwood Valley, California, 95470.

Raven's Call, A Quaint & Curious Volume of Forgotten Lore & Journal of the Old Religion; Moon Dragon Publications, Post Office Box 301831, Escondido, California, 92030.

Reclaiming Newsletter, published by Reclaiming: A Center for Feminist Spirituality; Post Office Box 14404, San Francisco, California, 94114.

Sage Woman: A Quarterly Magazine of Women's Spirituality; Post Office Box 641, Point Arena, California, 95468.

Solitary: By Choice or By Chance, published by the Re-formed Congregation of the Goddess; Post Office Box 6091, Madison, Wisconsin, 53716.

THE COVENANT OF UNITARIAN UNIVERSALIST PAGANS

SINCE ITS inception in 1985, CUUPS has served to strengthen the religious diversity embraced by the Unitarian Universalist Church. It is recognized as an Independent Affiliate Organization of the Unitarian Universalist Association, and many UU churches across the country have established chapters.

The following is a condensed list of the beliefs embraced by the Contemporary Pagans among the CUUPS membership, as originally published in their pamphlet, "Contemporary Paganism: Questions & Answers":

1. Divinity is immanent in all of Nature.

2. Divinity is just as likely to manifest in female form, as "the Goddess," the interconnectedness of life.

3. Multiple paths to the divine, as symbolized by many "Goddesses" and "Gods," often viewed as archetypes or gateways to the unconscious.

4. Respect and love for Mother Earth as "Gaia," a living being of which we are a part.

5. The goodness of creation, in which all beings are meant to live in joy, love, and harmony.

6. An ethics and morality based on the avoidance of harm to other beings and to the Earth, which mandates environmental activism as a religious responsibility.

7. The knowledge that human interdependence implies community cooperation.

8. The importance of celebrating solar and lunar cycles, and the cycles of our lives, leading to the revival of ancient customs (and the invention of new ones!).

9. A strong commitment to personal and planetary growth, evolution, and balance.

10. The awareness of making one's lifestyle consistent with one's beliefs ("the personal is political").

11. A minimum of dogma and a maximum of eclecticism.

12. A healthy skepticism and a reluctance to accept an idea without personally investigating it.

13. A distrust of would-be messiahs and gurus.

For additional information, contact:

The Covenant of Unitarian Universalist Pagans
Post Office Box 640
Cambridge, Massachusetts 02140

GLOSSARY OF TERMS

Altar: a table, stand, or demarcated space upon which ritual tools are arranged and around which members of a Circle sit or stand during celebrations

Athame: a knife used in ritual; should be newly forged and never have been used in hunting or combat

Beltane: holiday (Sabbat) celebrated the 1st of May; time of fertility and youth

Besom: a broom, particularly hand-made with twigs tied to a central rod

Chalice: a goblet or drinking cup

Circle: 1) the area in which Pagans meet for worship; 2) a group of people bound together by their common interest in and their celebration of spirituality; 3) a group of Witches who have not yet taken Covenstead; 4) verb, to Circle: the act of meeting together for worship

Consecrate: to make sacred by use of a ceremony; in Wicca, items are consecrated when they have been blessed by or immersed in the Four Elements and presented to the Gods in Circle

Coven: a group of Wiccans/Witches who have met together for at least a year-and-a-day and who have declared themselves a group practicing the Craft; see Starhawk's definition in *Why This Book Was Written, p. 3.*

Covenstead: a ceremony or celebration in which a group of Wiccans/Witches formally declare themselves to be a working Coven; a group will *take Covenstead* at the end of at least a year-and-a-day together

Craft, the: an umbrella term for all the traditions of Witchcraft; Wiccans/Witches practice the Craft

Crone: a woman who has achieved both age (generally 60+) and wisdom in her Craft life; also refers to the Goddess in her aspects as the Dark Moon, the Hag, the Reaper

Cult: in modern usage, a group which imposes its will upon its individual members to the detriment of their personal freedom; see the discussion of Cults in Chap.1

Dedication: a ceremony or vow to study the path to which one is called; in many Pagan traditions, a dedication is a formal ceremony in which an individual agrees to learn and a teacher agrees to teach

Dianic: a tradition of Paganism in which Deity is perceived as purely feminine, or in which only the female aspects of Deity are worshipped on a regular basis, or in which only women come together for worship

Drumming: a celebration or meeting in which drums and other instruments are played by all members in attendance

Eclectic: a belief system or practice drawn from many different sources or traditions; a Pagan/Wiccan/Witch may be referred to as an Eclectic if s/he uses many different pantheons or systems for her/his practice of the Craft

Equinox: occurs twice yearly; the day and night everywhere on Earth are equal because the Sun crosses the equator— in Spring, on or near March 21st is the Vernal Equinox (Wiccan Ostara) and in Fall, on or near September 22nd is the Autumnal Equinox (Wiccan Mabon)

Fam Trad: refers to a belief system said to have been handed down from generation to generation and to be closer to authentic Craft practices; an hereditary Witch is said to be one who practices the Fam Trad to which s/he was born or initiated

Handmaiden: generally the youngest female in the Circle whose responsibilities include sweeping the Circle and assisting the Priestess throughout the ritual

Hereditary: term referring to an individual who practices a tradition of the Craft which has been handed down in their family from generation to generation

Imbolc: Sabbat celebrated on February 2nd; also called Brigid or Candlemas; translates as "in the belly" and celebrates the time when animals are giving birth in their hibernation dens (in some traditions, the time when the Goddess returns from the underworld pregnant with the Sun God whom she births on Ostara; in other traditions, the Sun has been reborn on Yule)

Invocation: a formal prayer or request for the Gods and the Elements to be present in the worship space

Lammas: Sabbat celebrated the 1st of August; first harvest celebration

Litha: The Summer Solstice; this Sabbat celebrates Midsummer as well as the "marriage" of the Goddess and God in mythological terms

Mabon: The Fall Equinox, Sabbat said to be the Pagans' Thanksgiving—celebrates the fall harvest

Magic: the power to manifest change at will to bring life into a state of balance and harmony

Maid: a young woman who has not yet had a child and/or is not yet married; also refers to the Goddess as the New and Waxing Moon, the Nymph, the Virgin, and the Bride

Moon Lodge: a group or Circle which meets for worship on the Full and New Moons, generally a name associated with Dianic groups; refers to the menstrual hut of many ancient societies in which all women of a given village or area would reside during their menses

Mother: a woman who has had children or who is a maternal figure in the Circle or Coven (prior to the time of Croning); also refers to the Goddess in her aspects of motherhood—the Full or Pregnant Moon, the Hearth Keeper, the Nurturer and Caregiver

Occult: literally, hidden or concealed; has come to designate any and all esoteric arts, sciences, and studies

Ostara: The Spring Equinox, the Sabbat celebrating renewal and young life

Pagan: any person who practices any one of the religions of aboriginal peoples which have been supplanted by Christianity or a state religion

Pantheon: the Gods of a given people; i.e., the Celts, the Romans, etc.—the Celtic Pantheon would be all the Gods and Goddesses worshipped by the Celts

Polytheism: the belief in or worship of more than one God/Goddess

Priest: a man who serves as the ceremonial leader of a group gathered to worship

Priestess: a woman who serves as the ceremonial leader of a group gathered to worship

Ritual: the religious observance of ceremonial acts in the worship of Deity

Sabbat: any one of the eight Wiccan holidays: the Equinoxes (Spring & Fall), the Solstices (Summer & Winter), plus Samhain, Imbolc, Beltane, and Lammas

Samhain: the Sabbat celebrated October 31st; the Wiccan New Year and a time of introspection

Sistrum: a rattle or noisemaker

Skyclad: ritually nude; refers to being dressed appropriately for the worship of the Gods—having left all the mundane world behind; a symbol of freedom

Solitary: an individual who practices the Craft alone, without a Circle or Coven

Solstice: twice yearly, when the Sun appears to "stand still" and is the furthest from the equator; in the Northern Hemisphere, the Summer Solstice (Wiccan Litha), on or near June 21st, is the longest day of the year, and the Winter Solstice (Wiccan Yule), on or near December 22nd, is the longest night of the year. In the Southern Hemisphere, the events are reversed.

Spell: a focus of attention on a specific goal

Tradition: the particular type of Paganism or Witchcraft one practices

Wheel, the: generally refers to the Wheel of the Year, or the cycle of life-death-rebirth which is celebrated by the eight Wiccan Sabbats and the thirteen lunar cycles which comprise a year; the holidays themselves may represent different phases of the cycle based upon whether or not the tradition derives from a hunting or an agricultural society; one will often hear "The Hunting Calendar/Wheel" versus "The Agricultural Calendar/Wheel"

Wicca: the religion of modern Witches (most specificallly those from the British Isles)

Witch: any woman or man whose religion is any of the aboriginal European religions (the Old Religions)

Yule: The Winter Solstice; Sabbat celebrating the rebirth of the Sun in most traditions

The Crossing Press

publishes a full selection of titles
of general interest.
To receive our current catalog,
please call, toll free:
800/777-1048